Product Marketing: Effective Go To Market Strategy

Book Option

Published by Book Option, 2023.

Table of Contents

Copyright

Published by Book Option

Illinois 40432 USA.

Copyright © 2023 Book Option

All rights reserved.

Thank you for having an authorized edition of this book and for complying with copyright law. No part of this book may be reproduced, stored in a retrieval system, or transmitted by any means, electronic, mechanical, photocopying, recording, or otherwise, without written permission from the copyright holder.

Product Marketing: Effective Go To Market Strategy

Distributed by Book Option

For ordering information or special discounts for bulk purchases, please contact IngramSpark PO Box 14 Ingram Blvd, La Vergne, TN 37086 USA, 1-615-213-3525.

Design and composition by Book Option Cover design by Book Option For permission credits.

To offset the number of trees consumed in the printing of our books, Book Option donates a portion of the proceeds from each printing to the Arbor Day Foundation. Book Option has replaced over 500 trees since 2020.

First Edition

I dedicate this to the dreamers, healers, and givers who deliver value through art and invention, expression, and creation. With all my love.

About

The product marketing role is notoriously tricky to pin down and define. The type of product you market, stage of growth your company's at, industry you're in, and so much more, can impact how you execute your role.

This fundamentals class brings clarity to the product marketing position to ensure you're fully up-to-speed with what's an exciting and multi-faceted role, that sits at the interchapter of organizations large and small.

By the end, you'll walk away with a clear roadmap of the stages you need to nail to successfully get products to market - and keep them there, and a shorthand explanation of how to get the rest of your company to rally around your function.

Introduction

Introduction. In 1943, a naval engineer named Richard T Janes was stationed at Cramp Shipbuilding in Philadelphia and was tasked with designing the springs that would suspend delicate equipment on ships at sea, keeping them level in rough weather. As the story goes, he was experimenting with tension springs and dropped one hypnotized as the spring fell to the ground. Richard had an idea and the slinky was born.

Of course, that's not the whole story. That's the story of how a helical spring became a toy, not how the slinky as a product went on to sell over 300 million units before the year 2000. It is, in short, a story of invention. But for every product with an origin story, there's an equally compelling tale that doesn't get told the story of how that product makes it to market. In this book. We're not going to teach you how to invent the next iPhone or Slinky. Our mission is basic. We're going to teach you exactly how to take a new product to market.

Over the Book of our careers, we have launched countless new products and features for companies large and small, including Sony, PlayStation, Google backed rocket lawyer and multiple early and mid stage venture backed startups. We've also worked for agencies that have consulted for hundreds of small businesses on go to market strategies. This book teaches you how to apply the latest go to market tactics emerging from Silicon Valley, as well as the foundational strategic thinking from the Kellogg School of Management. We've broken the book into seven chapters outlined below, each one covering a key pillar of any go to market strategy. Within each chapter, we break each component into its foundational elements, cover tactical execution and pull examples from our experience taking products to market.

chapter one target audience. Who are you trying to target? How do you identify and segment your target audience? How do you know if you're at product market fit? chapter two Value Propositions Understanding Core Components of a value proposition, Competitive advantage positioning, unique selling proposition and value. Calculating product value with math. Defining value Propositions without Math. chapter three Messaging six Step Progress for Building Your Messaging Framework. Copywriting. How to do it plus four tips to do it well. chapter four. Go to a market team who's involved in bringing a product to market, choosing a team that suits your strategy.

Defining success metrics for your team. chapter five Demand Generation two Models for demand generation, an example of a demand gen campaign and seven common demand gen tactics. chapter six The Marketing Mix. Calculating the Marketing Mix. Building your Marketing Mix. chapter seven Price. The Basics of value based Pricing. Four. Common Pricing Tactics. By the end of this book, you'll understand exactly what you need to do to catapult yourself into the market and make your product the next slinky.

Target Audience Part 1

Part one: target audience who you target. This part of the book is all about the who of your go to market strategy. How to select your audience, what to look for in a good target audience, and how to link your audience to your overarching go to market goals. This chapter will cover how to set the business goal that your target audience is going to help you achieve the role that supply and demand plays in target audience definition. Common B2B and B2C segmentation tactics and strategies. How to size your market and product or market fit. Before you select an audience, set a clear numeric goal.

The big mistake managers make with going to market is jumping straight into the strategy without quantifying their desired outcome. The entire point of a strategy is that it's a means of achieving an objective. Without an objective, your go to market strategy is aimless. Starting with a strategy is a recipe for disaster. When I worked at Sony, I had identified the perfect target customer for a new product. It was a match made in heaven. The needs of the customer aligned perfectly with what the product delivered. The strategy was perfect, but there was just one huge problem. The customer segment was just too darn small. Even if I sold the product to every single member of that segment, it would barely have made a financial dent. You must have a goal such as a clear financial objective before you have a strategy.

In my case, my goal required an imperfect strategy that is pursuing an imperfect target customer because the goal was more important. Here are some examples of clear, quantified goals that will help dictate your strategy. Generate $15 Million in one year. Sell 100,000 units in six months. Break even on development costs in two years. Achieve 50% market share. Grow brand awareness among segment B by 90%. Grow purchase intent by 3% among Segment A. Grow Net Promoter score by 30% among current customers in Segment B. Generate $1 million in pipeline monthly recurring revenue or Mr.. Generate 200 qualified sales leads per month. Example, one of the most effective ways of generating new leads is to be a guest speaker for an influential organization.

I was reaching out to key organizations to schedule my CEO as a webinar speaker. This kind of marketing is very effective in building your company as an influential thought leader. The problem is that leads generated in this way can require a lot of nurturing before they are ready to buy. In the long term, such an approach makes sense. If your goal, however, is to generate X number of qualified leads this quarter, you shouldn't be wasting your time on high level long term content marketing. Your company could be burning through cash so quickly that it simply cannot afford to invest in long term tactics. Instead, the smarter Book of action is to focus on existing leads and get them to the point where they are ready to speak to sales reps. That requires building content that is a bit more product centric and that covers very specific pain points rather than high level aspirations.

Nothing will help you focus more than writing a clear numeric goal. You won't waste time on inconsequential tactics. You won't choose a target segment that is too small or too large. You will make smarter decisions on how to allocate your marketing budget. You'll be able to hone in on the partners who will matter most and you'll know what marketing budget to request. There's a reason you created this product, so it shouldn't be that hard to write down an objective. If you're working at a tiny company, your goal might be to retire off the proceeds from this product. In that case, just put down $3 million profit as the objective. That way you don't waste your time dealing with tiny markets and tiny marketing tactics. If you work for a large company, your goal might be to generate $100 Million in revenue or to acquire 1 million users without any clear financial target.

Just ask yourself one question. How will I know if this product was a success or not? Remember, if you're not the founder or CEO of the organization, make sure whatever goal you set aligns to the goal of the business. In larger organizations. The goal of the new product will be in part defined by the organization's needs. The number one way to do this is to ask what metrics are discussed in board meetings? What needles are the board of directors looking at and how will your product help move them? That's the best thing you can do to guarantee business alignment. Pick your target customer. I've worked with lots of companies that invested heavily in products only to see them fail miserably when they went to market. When it fails, people start playing the blame game. Our PR agent wasn't very good.

We didn't have the same features as our competitor. Google ads was a wasted investment. Onboarding was too slow and error prone. Another product released at the same time. The list is endless. But in reality, these are symptoms of a failed strategy rather than causes of the failed launch. Strategic mistakes cascade through everything, and usually a poor strategic decision results in tactics that don't work no matter what your budget. And the first strategic decision that usually gets made is choosing a target customer. If you choose the right customer, then you have a larger margin for error when it comes to executing your campaign. With that in mind, here's how you pick the right target customer. Estimate supply and demand. You need to select a target customer or market that has enough demand to achieve your desired outcome. This is a surprisingly common mistake. So let's break it down a little into the common traps we see. Scenario one no demand.

First, you have a product where there truly is not enough demand to support the primary goal. For example, let's say you're launching a new pet insurance product specifically for retired racing greyhounds. Great. That's a super niche audience, which means you can probably create a value proposition and messaging that's hyper relevant to your target customers. But let's say there are 2 million retired greyhounds out there and you need 4 million to achieve profitability. While your product might be great, there just isn't enough demand there to make the product work. If you're in this bucket, then you need to pivot to serve a larger target audience. Scenario two no demand yet. This is all too common in the world of technology. An entrepreneur identifies a problem and thinks I can fix this.

Currently, there's no market for their solution, but the potential market is huge and they're going to crack it wide open. This is called category creation, and if executed correctly, it can be extremely effective. Since you're all alone in the market, you tend to get a first mover advantage in all the perks that come with that, including brand awareness, thought leadership and zero competitors. However, category creation is extremely difficult. There are years of zero or no profit in revenue and you are usually required to spend huge sums of money on demand creation. That is educating people about the problem you've identified, creating a demand for your solution. Only then can you start the process of demand generation and start to see returns on your marketing spend.

More importantly, category creation is a long haul play, and if your product isn't sufficiently unique, you may find that your years of creating demand can be stolen by a newer, faster moving competitor who swoops in once you've done the hard yards of category creation. Scenario three. A lot of demand, but a lot more supply. Another big mistake would be selling something that is oversupplied. If you market something that doesn't provide much superior value over similar products on the market, then you are doomed to failure. This is why measuring supply is an important step in planning your go to market strategy. Example, one of the biggest mistakes new Amazon sellers make is choosing overly niche products that generate minuscule revenue. A smarter approach would be to look at what is already selling well, using data from a resource such as Jungle Scout and improve upon deficiencies that appear in product reviews.

Example, publishers have the very difficult task of trying to estimate how well a new book, video game, movie or similar product will perform in the market. This is particularly important because the bulk of the marketing budget is spent in one very narrow window of time. The way they overcome this challenge is by using comps or comparable products to see how well they perform historically. If you're selling a new product, look at how well similar products have done in the past to estimate demand. There are various ways to estimate demand and supply.

Look at how well comparable products are selling using tools such as Jungle Scout or your own historical records. Use Google keyword planner to see how many people are searching for a solution to the problem you sell. Google Trends can help if you expect demand to grow or shrink.

Target Audience Part 2

Identify your target market. More goes into picking a market than just making sure you have enough supply. Usually when marketers talk about target markets, what they're really thinking about are target customers. But this isn't quite accurate because markets include more than just customers. Imagine for a moment a physical marketplace, a place where people go to buy vegetables, clothing and tools. There aren't just customers in that market. It is an entire ecosystem of buyers and sellers. Focusing only on customers will get you into trouble. Airbnb, for example, cannot just focus on its target customers.

It must also create value for the many people who rent out their homes. That is, it must also focus on the sellers in the marketplace. Otherwise, the entire two sided market would fall apart and their marketing strategy would be unsustainable. A given target market actually consists of five components known as the five C's. One customer. Who are you selling to? What problem do they have? Two companies. In other words, your company. How do you solve your customers' problems? Where can you solve it better than the status quo or current solutions? Where can you solve it better than the status quo or current solutions? Three. Collaborators such as Partners and influencers. Are you relying on partners, resellers or platforms to help you get your product into the hands of your target customer? For context, such as changing the environment and regulations. Is there a compelling event that's driving a purchase now or are there regulations you need to work around?

Five competitors. Who else is in the market? Where do you win and where do they lose? How do people solve the problem right now? A note on competitors. When we talk about competitors, we usually think about other providers of our product. For instance, if you're making a movie for Netflix, you might think of your competitors as all the other movies on Netflix. In reality, though, your competitors are every single other way that your target audience can spend their leisure time. This might be playing video games, going to a movie, watching videos on YouTube, reading a book. It's endless. Another example is B2B software. While you might have competitors who people look at if they're considering your solution, your competitors are also how else they might solve the problem, which includes using software like Excel. Getting consultants to do it or just not solving it at all.

When you're thinking of competitors, you need to consider a much larger picture than just your category. As you can see, choosing a target market is more involved than simply finding the ideal buyer. It requires studying the overall market and determining whether that is a space where you want to participate. The customers in a particular market may be ideal, but if there are too many competitors active in the space, then it may not be viable. Alternatively, a particular market may seem unattractive because it has a lot of competitors, but if you happen to have collaborators with a lot of clout in that market, then it could be strategically viable. As you design your go to market strategy, it's important to consider all of the five C's, even if only in passing. Segmentation.

As you build your go to market strategy, one of the first questions should be who's going to buy this? And that's a more complicated question than you might think. There are dozens of different ways to define your target audience. Which strategy you choose will depend on your specific circumstances. But here are some tactics you can use to define your ideal client profile or ICP. From a graph in business to business marketing, it is common to divide customers based on their industry because in this case your customer is actually an entire business. Behaviorally, that is, you divide customers based on certain behaviors, such as how much money they spend or how much time they spend using your product.

It is very important to focus on your most profitable segments. Motivationally Overall, we would say that the best approach to segmentation is motivational. That is, you separate your customers based on their motivations for using your product. Demographic segmentation based on demographic information like gender and age. These approaches to segmentation are not mutually exclusive. You can actually combine them or use different ones for different purposes, one for strategy and another for media buying. For example, Most marketers rely on their intuition and arbitrary choices to segment the market. Often they don't realize they're doing this because they use quantitative data, which makes them feel as though they're being objective. Wrong. Quantitative data does not make your segmentation objective. Usually marketers segment based on industry, gender usage behavior or some combination of variables.

The problem is, they've predetermined which variables are important. How do you actually know that you should be slicing and dicing the market by industry or by gender? Why not by age or by income or by time spent using the product or by time of day using the product? How do you know which variables are most important to divide the market? In marketing. Today we're drowning in data. Because of this, you cannot look at the numbers and get an intuitive sense of what's happening. It's impossible. Humans are just too simple to see patterns in massive quantities of data. There's just too much complexity. That's where cluster analysis enters the picture. Cluster analysis. Cluster analysis is one way to systematically approach segmentation and use data to drive your audience targeting, thus laying the foundation for everything else in your go to market plan. Here's how it works.

First you collect your raw data. For instance, you might send out a survey asking lots of questions about people's behaviors and motivations when it comes to the type of product you sell. You might ask about firmographic and or demographic information, behavioral information or motivational information. For example, what were you doing when you decided you wanted to buy a product in this category? Then you take the quantitative results and run a statistical process called a cluster analysis. This process automatically clusters all of the data you've collected into segments. Once you have the groups, you can see if those groups correlate to demographic or firmographic data. For example, Group one might consist of people who spend a lot of time and money on their laptops. That group could also be predominantly male. While the group is determined by the continuous variables, time and money. It correlates positively with the binary variable gender.

A common go to market mistake is segmenting first with demographic or firmographic data when other data are often more relevant and easier to quantify. You're lucky if your segments align closely with demographic data because that makes targeting easier. Quite often, however, demographic data proves to be irrelevant. Usually customers segment based on needs that cross demographic and firmographic boundaries. At the end of this process, you'll have a statistically relevant map of insights. For example, say you're a software company who makes a data aggregation tool that syncs the sales and marketing tech stack and pulls out relevant data insights. Once you complete your cluster analysis, you might find that mid-market companies start to look for a product in your category when they're trying to push for a series B round of funding and need to pass stringent due diligence. Motivational. Use this way.

Cluster analysis can be a powerful way to segment and to choose your target customers. I am looking at a picture of a chart at the top of the title, says Dendrogram for Class A Cluster analysis. On the y axis. There's numbers going from 0 to 5000, 10,000, 15,020 thousand and are labeled L2 squared. Dissimilarity measure on the x axis is various abbreviations. The chart itself looks like a bunch of squares that are leading to each other and the reference is labeled fill enter. This is a visualization of what cluster analysis looks like. You can see here that there are basically three different clusters of customers. Cluster analysis accounts for many different variables. So it's not easy to make simple statements such as Cluster One is rich people and cluster two is poor people. You need to look closer at the data to see how the clusters differ from one another on each variable.

The specifics of how to do a cluster analysis will vary depending on which program you are using, such as SPSS or Stata. This work is absolutely critical to going to market. If you can understand the best people to buy your product, then you're going to be much more successful as you grow and spend your way into the market. How to do cluster analysis. Cluster analysis doesn't have to be some intimidating process that requires business intelligence tools and a master's degree in statistics. Here's how you can cluster your data using Excel and your CRM or system of record. Let's say you have data for 1000 customers. This includes hard data from your accounting system or Salesforce or wherever that tells you how much revenue these customers generate for the company.

Product usage data versus Pendo or a similar tool. Purchase history for each individual customer. And marketing data like participation in various campaigns or referrals you've received from them. There are countless behavioral metrics you could be collecting. All this data exists in your database, but you might also have tons of data from surveys that tell you things like what motivates them to buy in your category or what keeps them up at night. How do you make sense of it all? First, pull all the data out of your various systems and plonk it into a spreadsheet. Assign the first column in your spreadsheet to your customers. Every column thereafter should represent the variables you've collected for each customer. For example, your second column might be revenue, and your third column might be time spent using your product per month. Now you might start to see a problem here.

Each variable is on a different scale. For instance, how are you supposed to compare revenue to time? If your revenue is measured in millions of dollars and your time is measured in dozens of hours? Then the analysis is going to give undue weight towards the millions of dollars. That's why you need to standardize the data. One way to do this is to convert each data point into a Z score. By converting each data point into a Z score, you can fairly compare the numbers. The way you get a Z score is by taking your number, subtracting the average and then dividing by the standard deviation. You can learn more about this on Khan Academy. So let's take the revenue column. You need to calculate the average revenue for all your customers, followed by the standard deviation. By doing so, you can then replace every dollar figure with the Z score. Next, do the same thing for the time column.

Convert every time data point into a Z score. Another problem you're going to run into is that some of your variables are going to be binary, such as sex or non continuous, such as state or country. One way to handle these variables is to simply omit them from the cluster analysis. Once you've produced the clusters, you can then determine if those clusters correlate with anything like sex or country. Once you have a spreadsheet with your customer data standardized, you can run cluster analysis using Stata, SPSS, R, Excel or some other statistical program.

These programs will give you the option of producing a visual graphic. Here you can see how your customer data tends to group into clusters. The output of your cluster analysis might yield something like this. Suppose it generates four clusters. Cluster one tends to be high in revenue, but low on time.

Cluster two might be low in revenue and low on time. Cluster three might be high in revenue and high on time. And cluster four might be low in revenue and high on time. You can then run a correlation test between each cluster and the variables we couldn't test earlier, such as sex or country. You might find that cluster one tends to be skewed towards male. So let's take cluster one as an example. This group is high in revenue generated, low on time spent using your product and tends to be male. This could be the statistical foundation for a persona. Using cluster analysis, you can pull together disparate data threads to tell a story that you can use in your marketing. And by identifying different variables that tend to correlate to profitable customers, you can spend your marketing dollars efficiently by appealing only to those who are going to actually make your organization money.

Target Audience Part 3

Look at your most profitable customers. One of the easiest ways to choose a target customer group is to identify who your top customers are. Take a look at your accounting software or CRM. List your clients in order from the most profitable to the least profitable. You may also need to make some assumptions depending on how sophisticated your record keeping is. For example, you might need to use revenue as a proxy for profit. Here's an actual example of a case I worked on. The company had a software system to collect information on transactions and customers. I exported this to excel and then sorted the customers in order of the amount of sales they generated. If you have thousands of customers, I recommend that you break the data up into decimals.

By this I mean ten groups. So the first decimal will be the top 10% of customers in terms of revenue or profit. And the last decimal will be the bottom 10% of customers. Based on the statistical analysis I've done personally and the research I've seen. Your profit is probably being driven by a small group of clients. 80% of your profit could be coming from just about 20% of your entire client base. This is the same case I described earlier. Instead of presenting every single customer, I'm presenting ten clumps of customers. I took the total number of customers and divided that number by ten. That gave me the size of each vessel, and then I added up the sales for each vessel. I then divided that number by the total sales to the percentage of sales coming from that vessel to arrive at the cumulative percentage of sales. I just added up the numbers from the third column.

So what does this data tell us? Well, it shows us that almost 37% of sales are coming from just the first vessel. The first vessels account for half the sales. This has huge strategic implications. If over half your sales are coming from just 20% of your customers, then you may want to consider focusing just on that group. The remaining group might not be worth the effort. If you can get more people who look like that top 20%, then you may grow a lot faster. Now that you know where your revenue is coming from, you can do a cluster analysis and see what unites these customers. You want to ask what issues were they facing when they came to you? What complaints do they have? Why do they keep coming back to you? What compelling event drove their purchase? Segmenting without historic data.

The position a lot of start ups end in is having to make a lot of decisions around target market definition without a lot of existing data. When this happens, especially if it's a very early stage, they go back to selling to the audience they know rather than the audience that is the best fit for the product. Alternatively, they don't define the ICP accurately and try to target everyone. Neither is a good solution. Here's what you can do if you don't have any data. Talk to prospects. Identify where in the market there is evidence of underserved customers. And try to answer these important questions and take action from there. Where's your existing domain expertise? Can you use that to accelerate sales in a specific domain? And is it valuable to tap a local network first?

Personas. Once you've identified your target market with or without data, you need to make a decision on personas. Personas are essentially a person you've created that represents your target buyer.

The idea is you take your chosen company segment, identify who at that company is going to be the one who buys your product and you create a person to represent them. For example, if you sell mid-sized engineers to order companies and the person at your target organization who's involved in every deal is the director of mechanical engineering. Your persona might be mechanical, Mike. You layer on the demographic information that you know about mechanical Mike. Male, white, 45 to 67 years old. Married. ET cetera. Then the motivational drivers, for example, want to do a great job. Lots of pride in his work. Then the stressors and pains don't have enough time. Hard to balance time at the office with time with his family. Lots of experience, but not a big fan of change. ET cetera.

Finally, you'd package all of this information into a cheat card so anyone in the organization can understand your target audience. Personas can be powerful tools, particularly when they're based on data. It's often easier to create compelling campaigns. When you have a physical representation of the people you're actually selling to. Instead of engineering companies with over $50 Million in Annual revenue. However, be warned, personas take an extremely long time to craft. Well, if you're strapped for resources, then there are usually other go to market priorities that should take precedence. The only thing worse than no persona is an inaccurate one. And marketing is often guilty of building personas that don't meaningfully help sales teams or lead to creativity. That forges a meaningful connection with the audience. Because of the creative flair needed to craft a great sticky persona, they often become traps for what marketing teams suspect or wish their audience was, rather than a useful reflection of what it actually is. Market sizing.

However you decide to segment your audience, the next thing you need to do is figure out the size of this target audience to make sure it's big enough to reach your objective. This is called market sizing. Basically, are there enough of your target customers out there who can buy your product? Total addressable market. Tam. One of the best and easiest ways to market size is looking at the investor relations pages for public companies in your industry. Quite often public companies will post investor presentations that do the work of sizing the market for you. Often this is communicated in terms of a Tam or total addressable market. For example, if you work in e-commerce, look at the information Amazon and Shopify publish for their investors. If you work in creative software, look to Adobe. Another way to size markets is to look at databases of lead lists. If you work in demand generation, you may have purchased access to a database of companies or leads. You can plug in the criteria you're looking for, such as revenue, size and location, and the database will spit out how many companies fit that profile?

Keep in mind that the number you will get will only represent a fraction of the market. Unless your database has every company in the industry. So you will need to inflate whatever number you get. Ask whoever manages the database to estimate how much of the market the database covers. If the estimate is 75%, then you'll need to extrapolate by dividing your numbers by 0.75. A third approach to market sizing is to use the data companies provide you for free in their advertising platforms. When you sign up for advertising with LinkedIn and Facebook, for example, they will tell you how many people or companies fit the profile that you're looking for. You can use these numbers to estimate how many customers are in your target market. You can also do the same title based sizing based on government, census and labor statistics data. If you're targeting an international market, though, this process quickly becomes extremely time consuming and difficult. The fourth approach to market sizing is to look at third party research.

A research company may have already sized the market. Just look on Google and leverage the research that's already been done. The last approach to sizing markets is to do your own primary research. You could go out and manually count people, products or companies and then extract the sample you collected to the overall population. You could also do surveys and extrapolate your data in the same way. Keep in mind that there are a variety of different metrics that can be used to size markets. One is revenues or profits within a market. This information can come from different sources, including statista. Investor Relations pages or from market research companies such as Mintel. Another metric could be the number of companies or consumers, depending on your industry.

Other metrics may be even more important, such as order volume or pounds of material shipped. Serviceable, attainable market. Sam, if your Tam is the total number of customers who could potentially buy your product, then your serviceable, attainable market or Sam is all the customers who could potentially buy your product that you can actually sell to. For example, if you make whistles, your Team might be in the global whistle market. But if you can only serve as customers in the US, then your Sam would be the US whistle market. Sam is usually geographic, but it doesn't have to be. You might sell design software, but only support English. Therefore, your Sam would be the English speaking design world. Serviceable obtainable market somme.

Finally, some of your serviceable obtainable market is the chapter of the market you can reasonably target and who you can expect to purchase your product. Your segmentation work from earlier or any other work you've used to identify your target market should comprise your Somme. As a good rule of thumb, your Somme should be at least twice as big as your revenue objective in a given time period. For example, if your goal is to close $10 Million in revenue this year, then the Somme you need to do that needs to be at least 20 million. That's because you'll start to see diminishing returns once you reach 50% market share. As Jeffrey Amoore explains in Crossing the Chasm. Once you hit the halfway point, capturing the remaining 50% of a market becomes more trouble than it's worth. Instead, you should tweak your go to market strategy, relaunch into a new market, and do it all over again with all the lessons you've learned. This is called the beachhead technique. Pivot, pivot the harsh reality of diminishing returns.

All this work that you've now put in audience identification and segmentation comes with a vicious caveat. You're going to be doing it all over again and soon. Why? Diminishing returns. Diminishing returns are when your advertising dollars achieve progressively worse results for the same spend. Let's say you spend $1 million building awareness for your brand. Your brand awareness. In other words, how familiar people are with your brand will undoubtedly grow, but it's actually very difficult and expensive to go from high brand awareness to very high brand awareness. So you may want to identify where that inflection point is. Here's an example. In month one, your advertising spend was zero. Your brand awareness among targets was 0%.

In month two, your advertising spend was $100,000 and your brand awareness among target was 3%. In month three, your advertising spend was $100,000 and your brand awareness among target was 5%. In month four, your advertising spend was $100,000 and your brand awareness among target was 6%. You can see that if you spend nothing on advertising, you won't have any brand awareness. But let's say that you start spending the same amount on advertising each month. Your brand awareness jumps to 3% in month two and then to 5% in month three. But in a month for your brand, awareness only increases from 5% to 6%. You've invested the exact same amount, but you're getting less return for that investment. I took part of that table and pasted it into Excel.

I then inserted a graph to be able to see this visually. Do you notice how the orange line gets less and less steep? That shows the diminishing returns you face with this brand campaign and under that is a picture demonstrating that there is an orange line that goes up steeply, but then starts to level out and flatten. You need to decide as a team when it's time to pivot to maximize your returns.

Target Audience Part 4

Product lifestyle. As you can see, there are a lot of marketing decisions to make. And one critical factor is where you are in the product life cycle. Here you can see the typical stages in the sales curve that are used to depict the life cycle. I'm looking at a graph. On the y axis. It says annual sales volume on the x axis. It is divided up into four parts. One is introduction, two is growth, three is maturity or stabilization, and four is decline. And it's labeled as time. And the graph goes up slightly in introduction, a little bit more in growth. It plateaus in maturity or stabilization and then it goes down in decline. The reference is labeled Wiley and Sons.

A lot of thought. Leadership and marketing comes from people who manage products at the maturity stage. Often these products are consumer packaged goods from companies such as Procter and Gamble. At this stage, there's a strong emphasis on competition and cost cutting to drive up profit margins. There's also a heavy emphasis on massive brand marketing campaigns rather than demand generation campaigns. But for many go to market teams, the context is completely different. You might be working with products at the introduction and growth phases. At these stages, you often don't need to focus very much on competitors. That is because the market is growing and can support many different competitors.

Moreover, brand awareness may be so low that customers just aren't aware that you even have competitors. And on top of that, cost cutting may also be less important. One reason for this is that growth will come from other sources, such as expanding revenue in a growing market. Your target. In this case, early adopters are also often less price sensitive, so you can make up for high expenses with high prices. In these stages, massive brand marketing is less relevant. You and your competitors probably haven't built up the economies of scale required to invest in TV campaigns, for instance. It's also worth noting that in the early stages of a product's life cycle, it can be difficult to have a strategy at all.

The product may change rapidly to accommodate whatever market signals you receive. You don't have a lot of data on customers, and it's difficult to define what your target market really is. What's more, your value proposition may not even be all that different from your competitors. I'm a huge fan of strategy, but I must admit that in the early stages, trial and error can sometimes be more important than strategic planning. Identifying and analyzing competitors. A key factor in selecting a market is understanding the competition. This is a two step process. One: Finding your in-market competitors and two, finding and understanding your audience's competitive alternatives. Then you're in a good position to develop compelling value propositions and messaging to drive your go to market strategy. Step one: Identify your market competition.

This is probably the easiest step. The first kind of competition is the one we're familiar with. It's the companies and solutions you lose to after your target audience has decided to spend some money on the problem. So your first step is to identify who the competitors are within your chosen market category.

Sometimes this is easy. However, there are probably competitors who you're not thinking of or who you haven't run into during your sales cycles. Fortunately, there's lots of ways to get this information. Use tools like crayon to track competitors. Use tools like Spyfu, Google keyword Planner, Semrush or Moz to identify competitors based on their online content and advertising strategies. Look at category groupings on review sites like G2, Capterra, Yelp, or Google reviews. Hire people to research for you on Upwork or Fiverr. Review other organizations Web presences with tools like Similarweb. Review your existing data and identify who you're losing deals to. Does anything unite the deals you lose to specific competitors?

For example, size industry. ET cetera. And complete win loss analysis with your prospects. Who else did they look at during the sales cycle? Once you have a list of competitors, you need to start analyzing them. First look at the competitive advantage each competitor has. Competitive advantage basically boils down to just two things. One. Economies of scale. And two. Customer captivity. For example, churn rate estimate. Economies of scale. By collecting data on your competitors, such as the number of employees' revenue. Venture capital funding and social media followers. If you aggregate all of these, you can get a sense of their scale. To assess customer captivity, you want to look at things like subscription models, cancellation penalties, customization packages and personalization options for their products.

All these options make it more difficult for customers to leave. And from your perspective, that means your competitors are making it more difficult for you to capture their market share. After looking at competitive advantage at the economic level, I then look at competitors in terms of marketing strategy. Here you want to look at things like what target customers the competitors are going after and how they are communicating value to these customers. Look at their websites to see which verticals or industries they are targeting. Look at how they talk about their value proposition. You will get a sense of the positioning they are trying to use to secure the market. The third level I look at is tactical. Look at their pricing, packaging, product features, functionality and anything else that could be relevant, such as advertisements. The downside of this kind of analysis is that it can be endless. So you want to stay focused on the top competitors you've identified.

To find this kind of information. Start by scouring review sites and discussing these issues with your prospects. These conversations can be a gold mine for this kind of tactical information. By talking to people who have been through sales cycles with other companies, you start to get a sense for where those other companies focus and what they pitch as their value proposition. If you're lucky, you might even get a sense of how your prospects would respond to your product offering, and you can start to shore up your position against those objectives. The best way to help structure this analysis is a framework like the one below. This will give you an idea of market presence, quality of service and why people do or do not like them. I am looking at a sample table with seven rows and four columns.

The rows are labeled competitors. Domain authority. SEO Moz. Site Traffic Rank Similarweb Rating G2 Positioning from Reviews. Ease of Use G2 and specific product weakness. And the columns are labeled A, B and C. Competitor A has a domain authority of 47. A site traffic rank of 100,000. A rating of 4.0. Positioning from reviews is intuitive. Ease of use is 6.5. Specific product weakness is two times more expensive. Competitor B has a domain authority of 37. Site traffic rank of 500,000. A rating of 3.0 Positioning from reviews. Fast and easy ease of use is one specific product weakness that doesn't integrate to Salesforce. Competitor C has a domain authority of 55. Site traffic Rank of 900,000. Rating of 4.9. Positioning from reviews. Affordable. Ease of Use. 5.5. Specific product Weakness. Low Internal Adoption.

The first step is relatively straightforward. What's more challenging is mapping out your competitive alternatives. Step two: Identify your competitive alternatives. Competitive alternatives are what your audience would do if your product didn't exist. I like to think of it this way. If someone was solving the problem you solve without buying you or any of the competitors you've identified, how would they do it? For example, let's say you make marketing automation software. Your competitors might be HubSpot, Marketo and Pardot. Your competitive alternatives might be not doing email marketing, sending emails manually, or only running email marketing through sales cadences via the sales team. Or say, for example, you make running shoes specifically for running on treadmills.

Your competitors might be Nike and New Balance. Your competitive alternatives might be swimming. Other cardio gym activities like rowing machines, stair climbers. ET cetera.

Barefoot running or other less specialized footwear. Finally, let's say you're going to market with a new video game. Since you're primarily offering fun in exchange for time, your competitive alternatives are every other fun way someone could spend time. This includes other media such as TV, Netflix. ET cetera. Hanging out with friends or hobbies or classes. When you think about the customer life cycle, competitive alternatives tend to come first.

Before Netflix came along, for example, their customers were perfectly happy renting DVDs from a local store until Netflix convinced them that on demand streaming was what they really wanted. So the first thing you need to do is convince your target audience that they need what you're selling at all. Then once they're in the market, you need to convince them that your product is the best. Remember, you don't define the competition or the market your customers do. Which brings us to the issue of product market fit.

Target Audience Part 5

Product market fit. Marc Andreessen, the co-founder of Netscape and later the co-founder of Andreessen Horowitz, defines product market fit as being in a good market with a product that can satisfy that market. Essentially, product market fit means that a company has achieved three things. One, it has found a market for its product. Two, it has gotten that product into the hands of some of its target audience. And three, its customers are generally happy with the product and how it's solving their problem. In short, it's an amalgamation of everything we've talked about so far.

For startups, finding product market fit is critical. Put bluntly, if they fail to find product market fit, they'll fail completely. Even an amazing team with an amazing product has a small shot of success if it hasn't nailed its product market fit. But an average team with an average product with amazing product market fit will be incredibly successful. Therefore, before you go to market, it's essential that you have product market fit and that's going to look different depending on your organization.

For startups, it means you have secured some level of audience engagement, have a few customers under your belt and are generally getting positive feedback. You're likely reliant on founders selling and 1 to 2 great reps to get deals across the line. Landing a sale is still a big deal and a refined working sales process might not yet be in place. For larger organizations who are launching new products. Product market fit will likely be a different beast. Better brand recognition and an already proven market and a loyal audience all make it much easier to launch something new. However, those same benefits mean that your sales team, driven by quotas, will likely gravitate to your existing product line. What's more, your positioning messaging, target audience, sales, materials and competitors are likely all different from what your sales team knows. It's critical that you first secure product market fit that is selling a few deals, market testing your positioning, seeing if customers are happy before you really go to market and involve more resources.

Product market fit versus go to market. So what's the difference between finding product market fit and going to market scale? Product market fit is all about finding your target market with testing, iterating and exploring new ideas until you identify the people who are going to love your product and are enthusiastic to give you money for it. Finding product market fit is an inherently unscalable process because the focus is on riffing on new ideas incredibly quickly until you strike gold. It's also less focused on building a repeatable process because until you find your sweet spot, it's not worth the resources to make sure you can do it again and again. Go to market strategy, in contrast, is all about the ability to execute and convert your product market fit into repeatable, predictable revenue. Investing in people, processes and systems that mean you can reliably deliver on your revenue targets is the name of the game. And I'm looking at another table with two sides, a left and a right side. On the left side, it says Product market fit.

On the right side, it says go to market strategy. And it reads as follows Product market fit Founder VP sales involved on every deal. Go to market strategy. Executive leadership team is completely hands off on most sales product market fit sales process is loose Go to market strategy Sales processes buttoned down. Product market fit. Average contract value. Conversion rates and other core metrics are still in flux. Go to market strategy. Baseline metrics are well understood. ROI calculations produce predictable results. Product Market Fit focuses on MVP and I Iterative Product Sales Marketing Testing. Go to market strategy. Focus on processing optimization to lower customer acquisition cost. Product market fit testing takes precedence over execution.

Go to market strategy. Execution takes precedence over iteration. Product market fit inherently unscalable go to market strategy, endlessly scalable product market fit marketing is focused on defining audiences, positioning and messaging. Go to market strategy. Marketing is focused on generating demand within your target audience. Chapter Summary Questions. Is your target audience large enough to support your business goals?

Is there demand for your product beyond what the market is currently supplying, or are you creating demand for long term category domination? Have you identified your specific segments, including your Tam, Sam and Som? Do you know your competitors? Competitive alternatives. And have you positioned your product to win against both? Do you have product market fit?

Target Audience Takeaway

The single most important thing that I want you to remember from this chapter is that nothing matters more than the sheer size of your market. You can have perfect marketing execution. You can have a perfect value proposition. But if there just is not enough demand, you've completely wasted your time and resources.

One of the key things that distinguishes product marketing managers from conventional marketing managers is strategic focus. That means you're less concerned with perfect messaging. Less concern with perfect conversion rates. And you're much more concerned with the absolute potential market. That market potential is also the highest priority for potential investors. Moreover, at the end of the day, the single biggest competitive advantage that you could possibly have is economies of scale.

Value Proposition Part 1

Part two Value Propositions Understanding Your Value. Now that you know who you're targeting, you need to refine what your unique value proposition is for your go to market strategy. Your value proposition isn't an ad or a piece of marketing collateral. It's an internal tool to help the entire go to market team understand what you bring to the table for your target audience.

Collectively your segmentation value proposition and messaging, which we'll address in the next chapter form the foundational core of your entire go to market approach. In this chapter, we're going to define the key components that make up a value proposition. Explain how to calculate the dollar value of your product. Explore what to do if your value isn't attributable to a dollar figure. By the end of this chapter, you'll understand what a value proposition is, where it fits in your go to market strategy and how to find one for your own product. The value proposition. A value proposition is a fundamental component of your marketing strategy. It is all the benefits you are offering, all the ways you create value documented and outlined in a single place. It's an internal tool that will help focus your marketing on the value you bring to solve specific pains for your specific audience.

A good value proposition should be made up of three different components. Competitive advantage Positioning and USP. However, marketers often use these terms interchangeably when in fact they mean very different things. So we're going to dive into what each one is and how it relates to your value proposition. Of course, it's entirely possible to go to market without all three components. However, the strongest go to market strategy will be delivered by organizations who have multiple components in place. For example, if you have no competitive advantage over your next best alternative, but you have great positioning, you can successfully capture significant market share. However, you're going to be relatively easy to displace down the road. That's why we recommend when you're building your go to market strategy and your value proposition, you try to anchor it to as many components as possible.

This might mean you develop additional product features, target audiences or pricing and packaging configurations to check every value proposition box. Competitive advantage. Competitive advantage is an economic term. That means a condition or circumstance that puts a specific company in a superior business position. There are four common types of competitive advantages. One. Economies of scale. A company can produce more of their product at a lower cost because they're producing a lot of it, which makes it difficult for others to compete due to the low cost. A specific company can offer. Mass producing suits versus bespoke suits are an example of this, where the mass produced suit can offer a much better price and capture more of the market because of it, due to the fact that they're making lots of suits at once and thus paying less to make each one. To customer captivity.

The cost and resources of switching to a competitor are very high. So it's hard for customers to switch. B2B subscription software SaaS often rely on this since switching to another SaaS provider will likely require implementation. Data processes and people change, all of which are costly to the business and politically taxing internally for the people involved. Three enforced competitive advantages. Government licenses can prevent competitors from entering a market and offer a competitive advantage to those who hold the licenses. Telecommunications, infrastructure, transit and energy companies are often an example of this for technology advantage. When a company has developed a truly innovative product that is both patent protected or impossible to replicate.

Pharmaceutical companies are a good example of this sort of competitive advantage when they develop a new drug that can do what no one else can do. A word of warning about technology advantage. It's easy to fall back on technology as your competitive advantage, especially for tech companies. The reality, however, is that most technology companies do not in fact, have a technology advantage. Yes, they solve a problem in a unique way, but generally speaking, it's not sufficiently different from the next best alternative to be a true moat. There are exceptions, Of course, for legacy solutions. Moving to the cloud is incredibly resource intensive, if it's possible at all. So cloud first products have a significant moat. Another example is data gong. IO, for example, is a sales engagement and call recording solution for sales teams. Their technology records calls, so sales reps and managers can listen back on the call and coach sellers to improve.

However, that technology is very easy to replicate. So Goncalo created a competitive advantage with data and machine learning. They analyze all the calls of their customers, creating a huge database of sales calls and then use machine learning on those calls to build a world class recommendation engine. Their technology advantage isn't their product technology, but rather an advantage in data and machine learning, both of which are very difficult to replicate quickly. Unique selling proposition. USP Your unique selling proposition is the single reason that sets you apart from both the competition in your category and from the next best alternative. It should be the combination of a critical feature set, the benefit that the customer gets, and how that relates to the pain you solve for.

Of course, this is often very similar to your positioning as we'll see in a second. The difference is that your USP is highly specific. It's a single feature or feature set that sets you apart from everyone else. For example, if you were selling a gaming system, one unique value proposition might be exclusive rights to a specific game that is only available on your system. By honing in on a hyper specific feature, set or benefit, you make it very clear to your potential customers why they would buy you over someone else. It's a single thing you can point to and say, This is how we're different from everyone else. Defensible USP. One challenge that startups in particular have is finding a defensible USP. What we mean is that your USP must be inarguably unique to you. Ideally backed by data and social or third party proof.

For example, a lot of companies want to make customer service their USP because they're great at it and their customers love it.

But is that defensible? No. Unless you've won an award or been recognized by analysts like Forrester or Gartner, or you'd be the highest ranking company or something like G two. It's not something you can concretely say, We are the best. Plus, you'll have to look long and hard before you find a company who says we have terrible customer service. Rather, your USP should ideally be something your competitors say No, we don't do or have that. Otherwise it's extremely easy to counter in a head to head, and it makes it hard for the customer to understand why they should buy you instead of someone else.

Positioning. Finally positioning. Positioning is the choice about which aspect of your product you're going to focus on to add the most value to your target audience. In other words, positioning is about staking a claim to say this is who we are and how we help. If you don't want this, then our product is not for you. Of course, this is incredibly scary. You're actively saying our product is not for this type of customer, and we address this in more detail in the next chapter on messaging. For now, though, there are a few things about positioning that are worth calling out now. One Positioning is critical. You need to actively select what makes you unique. Two positioning often feels like it should be obvious, but it rarely is.

Remember, what gets you excited is probably not the same thing that gets your customers excited. Three positioning is as much about saying what you're not as what you are. It's tempting to be something for everyone, but that rarely works. For every product is positioned. Either it's done by you telling the world what you are and what you do, or it's done by the market, telling you who you are and what you do. Once you've identified these three core components, you can start to move on to the last step of outlining a value proposition. Actually calculating the value to customers of your solution.

Value Proposition Part 2

Value how customers benefit. Value is the dollar amount that customers get back when they buy your product. A simple example might be your product costs $100 and it saves your customers $500. Your value is $400. Value is usually very dry in mathematics and is something that you actually calculate. And there's a footnote here that says we'll cover UN incalculable value in the next chapter. For example, saving people thousands of dollars on lubricant costs per month or reducing their order processing time by one minute.

Even if your product doesn't actually save your customers money, it may still save them theoretical money. That is the money that they would otherwise have to spend if they didn't adopt your solution. Calculating Product Value. Calculating value can be complex, but the theory is simple. First, identify the cost of doing nothing. Continuing to live with the pain. Then calculate the cost plus benefit of solving the problem in a different way. This might be a competitor. Finally look at your own product. What's the cost of your product and what sort of return can your customers expect to get? Let's say your product is an energy efficient light bulb for factories compared to a regular light bulb. That is the cost of doing nothing. It might save your customers $10,000 per year in expenses. Your customer is also looking at other energy efficient light bulb providers. Your competitors.

Maybe your best competitor can save them $8,000 per year in expenses. If that's the case, your value is $2,000 over and above the next best alternative. This table lays all of the cost savings out. I'm looking at a table here. It says Cost savings, your competition and difference. And the categories are electricity. You are $10,000. Competition is $8,000. Difference is $2,000. Labor is $5,000. Competition is $6,000. Difference is negative one thousand dollars. Oil you is $1,000. Competition is $1,000. Difference is $0 total you are $16,000. Competition is $15,000. Difference is $1,000. So you're able to significantly lower their electricity costs, their labor costs and their oil costs compared to a regular light bulb. Compared to doing nothing. The value you add is $16,000 since you do have some competition. The value you offer compared to your next best alternative is $1,000. When it comes to value propositions, you need to look at your value compared to the next best alternative, since that's how the customer is going to look at it.

Your goal is to say we offer X amount of dollars of additional value compared to the next best solution to your problem. Let's look at another example. This is an actual value proposition I worked on for a software product. As the table shows, that value came from three main sources. Savings through inventory. Savings through automation and savings through returns and Itrillioneads Savings from reduced inventory. $375,000. Savings from automation. $59,904. Savings from fewer returns. Savings from fewer returns. $1,350,000. Product price. $22,360. As you can see, the most significant savings was through returns. In fact, it was so much larger than the other two that ItrillionEALLY helped us focus our USP and positioning on the problem that we solved really, really well.

Since we contributed so much value through reducing returns that became our core position in the market. In these two examples, the value comes directly from cost savings. But remember, there are a few different ways that a company can offer value. Cost saving is by no means the only one. For example, your value proposition might include incremental profits rather than just reduced costs. An incremental profit is the value that a customer gains when a product adds to their revenue. We use the term incremental here because for every dollar your product adds to revenue, it only adds a fraction of profits. So the value here is the incremental profit added. Why bother calculating value? Many marketers rely on messaging to drive value, focusing on what customers want to hear rather than focusing on where the product adds value. But as the examples above illustrate, a bit of math can help you to quantify the value that your product creates and your target market. And once you've done that, you'll have an easier time pitching to your target audience.

Let's say you're selling software that automates when lights turn on and off in big commercial buildings. How do you sell this to prospects? Automate your lighting. Save time with automatic lights. The best lighting software. There are many different approaches you could take with these headlines, and chances are that most would miss the mark. That's because you haven't actually identified the value that you are creating. You need to break it down. How does your software actually help the business? How does it affect the profit equation? Profit equals price minus cost multiplied by quantity. There are a few possibilities for how your software might drive value. Because the lights are automatic. That might mean that customers don't need to hire staff to go around turning lights on and off. That could cut costs. The lighting might foster a special mood in the building or a more pleasant customer experience. This could help boost revenues.

The lights might spend more time turned off reducing energy costs. When marketers do positioning, they often guess at which benefit is most important and build campaigns around that. But a more sophisticated approach is to actually calculate how much value is created from each possible benefit and run the one that offers the most value. So of the three benefits, let's say that lower energy cost is the one with the most value. Sure, the savings for an individual building might be marginal, but when these costs are scaled across ten or more buildings, the energy savings are substantial. Now we're honing in on the main benefit of the value proposition lowering the customer's energy costs along the way.

We've better defined the target customer. Companies with ten or more large stores or buildings. These prospects have substantial energy costs, so cutting expenses becomes more important. With this information, a company can put the most valuable benefit in this case, lower electric bills at the heart of its positioning, making a much stronger case for customers as it goes to market. What to do if you can't calculate value. Math is undoubtedly your friend when it comes to value propositions, but there are a raft of products that provide significant value that can't be calculated easily. Either the value isn't monetary at all or the value is intangible. It's not something you can easily attach a dollar figure to. This is particularly common for

B to C companies. For example, imagine you are marketing Coca Cola. Technically, for the customer, the dollar value is the calories and enjoyment. They're cheap. But Of course that's not how Coca Cola markets itself. Instead, the value it provides its customers is cool. It creates and markets an image of what a Coke drinker is, then sells the drink as the path to achieving the image they've created.

So if a dollar value is not part of your value proposition, you need to focus on compelling use cases for your target audience. What is the number one most important value that your product brings to the table, and why do they specifically want to access that value that your product brings? Let's go back to our Coca Cola example. If the value they provide is a cool image, then they might tailor that value to specific audiences. For example, if they were targeting grandparents, they might focus on how Coca Cola can help them connect with their grandkids because it's a cool drink. Conversely, if Coca-Cola was targeting teens, they might focus on how Coke can make you popular at school, since that's probably what cool means to teenagers. Your value proposition does not need to be unique. Here's a final note on value propositions. They don't always need to be unique.

Marketers spend a lot of time trying to figure out their USP, and this is certainly a worthwhile exercise. But you don't always need to emphasize how unique your product is. For example, you might be selling something that is a non strategic purchase such as plastic screws. Your buyer probably doesn't care what makes your product unique. They just want something reliable at a reasonable price. In this case, emphasizing uniqueness is a waste of time. Or let's say you're operating in a brand new innovative market. Your customers might have zero knowledge of your competitors. In a case like this, there's no point in emphasizing how you're different from your competitors. Instead, just focus on communicating how you create value. Chapter Summary Questions. Does your product create enough value for the customer to be worth buying? Have you identified your competitive advantage positioning and unique selling proposition?

Have you calculated the value you add to your customer and linked it to a specific benefit or feature? Have you tied your value calculation to your USP positioning and competitive advantage to build a complete and robust value proposition? Can the value you create be measured in dollars and cents? Or are you bringing a more nebulous concept of value to your customers? Have you identified the part of your product that brings the most value? 11. chapter Summary Exercise - Value Propositions Does your product create enough value for the customer to be worth buying? Have you identified your competitive advantage, positioning, and unique selling proposition?

Have you calculated the value you add to your customer, and linked it to a specific benefit / feature? Have you tied your value calculation to your USP, positioning, and competitive advantage to build a complete and robust value proposition? Can the value you create be measured in dollars and cents, or are you bringing a more nebulous concept of value to your customers? Have you identified the part of your product that brings the most value?

Value Propositions Takeaway

The main thing that I want you to remember from this chapter is that the primary function of marketing is to create and communicate value for customers, partners and your company.

The key is to get very specific about how exactly you create value, and often that's not apparent until you do some research. So, for example, by talking to customers or potential customers, by calculating and assigning a monetary value to each and every benefit or feature, and how much value you create is constrained strongly by how much value your competitors also create.

Messaging Part 1

Part three messaging. What to say and how to say it. Messaging is how you tell the world about your product. It answers the question, Why should I buy this? It bridges the gap between one positioning where you define what you sell, who you sell it to, and the value they get. And two demand generation or advertising where you tell the world about your product. If you have a tightly defined audience and a clear value proposition, you're in a good place to develop great messaging.

Great messaging tells your target audience what you do and why they should buy you. Use the language your target audience uses. The problem your audience has and drives action to solve it and communicates the value you provide. You want to build a messaging framework that gives you both the flexibility to play in multiple channels and across campaigns, but still stays laser focused on solving the problem you've defined. Your messaging framework should also work to positively build your brand equity. One question I get a lot is why bother with all of this? Our sales team knows what to say and who to say it to. It's a good question. Building a messaging framework is time consuming and can feel a little bit redundant. But the reality is that without a framework, your messaging will drift off Book as you run different campaigns, produce different pieces of content, and hire new sales reps for your growing go to market team.

To keep your product and your company moving in lock step towards your objective, you need to keep everyone on message all the time. And a messaging framework is the best tool to do that. The process I outlined for building a messaging framework in this chapter is based on the pragmatic marketing framework and the positioning book. Obviously awesome by April Dunford. I've used it to build messaging frameworks for complex B2B products and it works wonders for keeping your messaging focused. In what follows. We're going to walk through the six steps you need to go through to build a great messaging framework. Once we have those six steps down pat, the rest of the chapter will focus on copywriting. This is the other side of the messaging coin. If your messaging framework helps you work out what to say, copywriting is all about figuring out how to say it.

The copywriting chapter offers a few essential rules of thumb that will help you communicate effectively with your target audience. Building your marketing framework. Building a messaging framework can seem like a mammoth task, but it can effectively be broken down into six manageable steps. One: Find the features your audience cares about. To find the advantage of your selected features. Three Link your advantages to value. Four. Group the benefits you offer by themes. Five Map Values to Personas and build use Cases. And six build the framework. In this chapter, we take a deep dive into each of these steps, looking at why they matter and how to execute them effectively. Step one: Find the features your audience cares about. Your product has dozens of features. You need to list them all out, then select the ones your audience cares about. For instance, say you sell TVs. Your product has lots of features, including a black stand, a power cord, plug and play software, a remote and 4K resolution of these features.

It's pretty clear that the 4K resolution is the feature that the target audience is going to care about. Having a remote probably isn't going to convince anyone to buy. At the end of this step, you should have a refined feature list of things your product does that your audience actually cares about. There are a few ways to get this information. Talk to your existing customers, if any, about what features they love about your product or competing products. Review old support logs or call transcripts. Are there consistent requests to address a problem that your new product solves? Talk to your product owners. Why did they recommend building a feature in the first place? Step to find the advantages of your selected features. Now that you have your features, you need to define their advantages.

An advantage is why you included a specific feature. It's the positive outcome that your feature creates. If we go back to our TV example, the advantage of 4K resolution is crystal clear picture quality. Advantages should be relatively easy to come up with since you presumably built the product in a specific way for a specific reason. Step three: Link your advantages to value. People don't buy features or advantages. They buy the value or benefit that they get from your product. Value is the. So what of your product features and advantages? And if you can clearly communicate the value of your product and do it in the language of your target audience, your legions ahead of most go to market teams. Most messaging stops at advantages. That's because linking your features to value and benefits is extremely challenging. It requires deep customer knowledge as well as empathy to understand what they're struggling with.

What makes this doubly challenging for go to market teams is that they know the product so well, and when we know a product, we're generally very good at describing what it is and what it does, but not so good at describing why someone should care. It's so ingrained in us that it's hard to put into words. We lose the forest through the trees. The result is that most teams go to market with features and advantages and make the consumer create the value themselves. But it doesn't need to be this way. By forcing yourself to clearly delineate between advantages and value, you can chip away at your product to get to the core reason that someone would buy it. So how do you make this important distinction between advantages and value? The best way to move from advantages to benefits is to look at each advantage and ask, So what? Why does our audience care about this? Let's go back to our TV example. The feature is 4K resolution.

The advantage is crystal clear resolution. So what? Why should I care about the resolution? Well, the benefit is that you'll feel transported to whatever you're seeing on the screen. For some products, particularly heavy commoditized products with lots of competition, you might be able to rely on your audience to convert the advantage into a benefit themselves. That's why we often see ads for consumer tech products like headphones, cameras and TVs that simply spout features as though their clear advantages. For instance, a TV ad might just say 4K resolution in your living room. Or a camera ad might just say the new iPhone has a 12 megapixel camera. These products don't have to explain this. So what? Because consumers have enough context that they already know.

However, relying on this is a dangerous game. It makes it harder to differentiate your product as competitors, copy your features and advantages so it can leave you vulnerable to alternative providers. Your audience might only translate your features and advantages in one specific way, whereas you might be able to think of more and more compelling value. One of the best ways to get from advantages to value is to talk to your target audience. Listen for what they complain about, don't like, or struggle with.

What do they wish was different in their professional or personal lives? And where do those wants overlap with your solution? These sorts of discussions can give you the insight you need to get to your products. So what? At the end of this stage, you should have a table that looks like this. On the Leftmost side feature, what does the product do? In the middle. Advantages. What's the advantage for our target audience? And the rightmost side value. So what? Why does our audience care?

Messaging Part 2

Step four Group The Benefits You Offer by theme. As you build out your benefits, you'll likely see some themes emerge. That is, multiple advantages, and features usually lead to similar benefits or benefits tied together neatly into a package. Therefore, the next step is focused on codifying lots and lots of values into a few major buckets. As you begin to go to market, you'll see which segments of your audience respond best to which theme and can tailor your campaigns accordingly. Step five: Map values to Personas and build use Cases.

You need to map everything you've done to your target personas. If you didn't build target personas, simply map them to the relevant people in your buying committee. The group of titles usually involved in your deals. Take your themes and see where they fit most effectively. Naturally, this matching will change as you go to market and learn what's working and what isn't. But it's good to have a starting point. It's also valuable to create use cases that map to your personas. If you know the value you deliver, how is the use case of that value different for different personas? Take our TV again. The value is that it transports you to whatever you're seeing on the screen. That's a great start, but it's pretty generic.

To make it more compelling. You can tailor it to personas with use cases for each one. For instance, if a segment you're targeting is sports fans, the use case might be to transport yourself to the big game. It's essentially the same value. It's just reframed to suit the audience. Step six: Build the framework.

Your final step is to put all of this in a framework which you can use to understand what you say, why you say it, and to whom. It's also helpful at this stage to create short summaries of your product. I like a one sentence summary. A two sentence summary and a five sentence summary. These summaries are surprisingly useful, both as an exercise to condense all the work you've done down into something very small, but also as an asset to have on hand. They always come in handy.

Reps can draw on them when they're practicing their elevator pitch. You can drop them into bios of executives if you're featured in the news, and they can even act as a functional anchor to keep discussions about your messaging tight. You might be thinking that this is a lot of work to end up where you already are, but building your messaging framework and putting it down on paper in this concrete way is critical. It not only makes your messaging a lot easier for other internal teams to consume and understand. It also forces you to confront your thinking about why a specific benefit is important and what feature set best tells the story of that benefit. It's also worth noting that although you'll build your framework from features down to use cases, your framework should operate in the opposite direction. So when you put your framework into practice, you should be focusing on the granular specific value that you bring to your customers first before diving into how you do it. Which are the advantages and what you actually sell?

Which are the features? Once this final step is complete, you're ready to tackle copywriting. Your messaging framework has successfully set out what to say. Now it's time to figure out how to say it. That's where copywriting comes in. Copywriting.

It's impossible to talk about messaging without talking about copywriting. Copywriting is how your messaging makes its way out into the world. Of all the parts of go to market strategy, copywriting is probably the most misunderstood. Often when people hear copywriting, they imagine Don Draper dreaming up slogans like it's toasted on the spot for clients. They picture creative agencies coming up with things like Got milk or What's up or because you're worth it. In reality, though, copywriting is about communicating the value of your product to your audience as clearly as possible in a way that compels action.

It might be super creative and innovative, but it also might not. Often effective copywriting is really straightforward. Here are five rules of thumb to help you as you communicate with your target audience. Number one, speak directly to the buyer and do it conversationally. Some of the strongest words in copywriting are words like you and your. You want to speak directly to the buyer as you would in a one on one conversation, and you want to do it in a language that they use every day. To achieve this, try to follow these four guidelines. One. Use a conversational tone. This means avoiding academic professional speech that is overly formal or grammatically correct. For example, writing such as might be grammatically correct when you're about to list some examples. But in reality most people would simply say like. Generally the best copywriting has a more informal conversational ring to it. To write in the second person as though you were speaking directly to the buyer.

For example, automating your accounting is better than automation for accounting. It's more personal. It speaks more directly to the audience and it's also more compelling and direct. You're telling your audience what they specifically will be able to do once they buy your awesome product. Three write in the present tense. This takes the abstract future benefit and makes it seem more tangible. For example, getting a girlfriend is better than getting a girlfriend or having a girlfriend. Note here the use of the imperative mood writing in a way that commands or requests. For right in the active tense.

Technically, this means that the subject performs the action of the verb in a sentence, rather than the subject being acted upon by the verb. For those of you who aren't active members of the grammar police, this basically means that your writing is going to have a lot more impact. For example, getting 10% off has a lot more power than 10% off will have by you. One of the easiest rules of thumb is this: avoid the words be and by in your copywriting. It won't work all the time, but it'll help a lot.

Messaging Part 3

Number two. Witty, brief headlines usually aren't effective. Keep it straightforward. Ads that try to be clever are rarely effective. Most of the time it's better to go with a more direct headline that communicates how your product creates value. There are a huge number of meaningless headlines out there that try to be brief or clever. You know, the ones maybe there's a period after each and every word or some abstract joke posted on a billboard. But here's the thing that you've probably noticed. These ads don't usually drive you towards a desired action.

At best, they give you a chuckle and make you feel warm and fuzzy about the brand behind them. In general, it's better to just get to the core of how your product creates value. You can do this by focusing on the outcomes that the customer wants. For example, double your income in one year or save $10,000 in energy costs. These headlines communicate the value achieved from whatever it is that you're selling. When it comes to writing headlines. Another thing we advise is to write in the sentence case that is capitalizing only the first word of the headline and proper nouns. This lets you write longer, clearer headlines and it'll help you avoid short, witty and confusing ones. Number three Cheesy, salesy writing works.

At the tactical level. I think most of us have lost the art of sales copywriting over the past few decades. It seems marketers have fallen into the habit of producing copywriting that reads well and is even a bit formal at the expense of salesmanship. But the truth is, cheesy, salesy writing works better. John Capel proves the effectiveness of this style in his books making ads pay and tested advertising methods. The modern demand generation guru Howard Sewell also demonstrates this in his article. But wait, there's more. Why does a cheesy copy still work? So what kind of writing is effective? Phrases like, But wait, there's more. Use of the ellipsis instead of proper sentences so that the reader is encouraged to keep reading. Short, punchy sentences. Incorporation of enthusiasm.

Many writers seem to lack. Enthusiasm in their writing. Promising quick results. Phrases like announcing. Introducing new and free. Making specific promises such as you will make $100,000. Remember, these phrases will be different depending on what you're selling. Being salesy only works if your sales offer is something that your audience wants. Number four stays on brand. Staying on brand means using language that is consistent with the brand, and this is one of the most important considerations in effective copywriting. Many companies will have a brand guide, but if not, you may need to make one from scratch in order to keep your copywriting on brand and on message.

The brand guide should outline what kind of personality your brand has, and it may even go into detail about the specific type of copywriting that you should be trying to execute. Here's an example where brand compliance is important. This is an ad for Metromile. Notice the funny poetry in the beginning and use of the word. Ta da! This is a very casual and friendly brand. It sounds as though Metromile wants to be your friend. Roses are red pay per mile. Car insurance could cut your bill in half. Ta da! If you are writing messages for this brand, you'd want to be consistent and use this chummy language. This is important because consistency will help to build a strong brand position in your customer's mind. Inconsistency, on the other hand, dilutes your brand positioning.

Brand guides can get much more specific than this. They might even include some complete phrases that you can pull. Each feature might have key bullet points that have already been vetted by copywriters or executives in your company. Number five. Be persuasive. We can't overstate how important this is. Think back to our definition earlier. Copywriting is communicating the value of your product to your audience as clearly as possible in a way that compels action. That last piece compels action is key, but it often gets forgotten. Copywriting is fundamentally about changing behavior that could be persuading prospects to buy a product, use a feature, click a button, believe in your company, or to take some sort of action. The thought leader on persuasion is the professor Robert Cialdini, who is famous for his book Influence. These are his key drivers of persuasion. Scarcity. People are motivated to take action if they believe something is scarce.

For example, using the phrase three days left persuades people to act because whatever you're offering is only available for three days. If it were available all the time. There's no sense of urgency. People prioritize things that are time sensitive. People don't like missing out. Consensus. People are motivated to do things if they believe other people are doing that same thing. Social proof is an incredibly strong, persuasive tactic. A good example of this is 90% of people prefer if 90% of people prefer this option, then the user will likely choose that action. Some people are nonconformist, Of course, but the vast majority of people rely on consensus or social proof to make decisions. This is particularly true in situations where the user isn't informed enough to make a decision on his or her own. Authority. People are persuaded if someone in a position of authority tells them to do something. Using phrases such as Dr. Joe Stevens or the expert in this field will persuade people. Reciprocity is also an important consideration.

As humans, we have a compulsion to reciprocate when we are given something. Giving people something for free could motivate people to take action in return. Consistency. People want to be consistent. If they told you something in the past, they want their future actions to be consistent with what they said. You could remind people of what they did in the past by using phrases such as Since you enjoyed. This may prompt people to buy something or take an action consistent with past actions. Lastly, people are persuaded by things they like using. Cheesy phrases such as You are awesome, can give your product more persuasive power. User experiences with this type of language can be particularly pleasant. Flattery is a powerful tool for building your brand personality and giving your brand product persuasive power.

Messaging Part 4

Copywriting example. This example of messaging helps illustrate some of the major copywriting rules of thumb that we've covered in this chapter. The ad reads. Weekend Sale. Put your dreams first today and learn for only 28.99 Canadian one day left. Let's start with persuasion. This is really emphasizing a sense of urgency by using scarcity. One day left for the weekend sale.

Put your dreams first today. They're not drawing on other persuasion tactics like consensus or authority, but there are hints of liking here. Put your dreams first, for example. People tend to like it when conversations center around them and you are also important here. Personalization itself is a useful tool for persuasion. This messaging also highlights an important point. Not every message you write needs to use every tactic at once, but good messaging will usually use at least one. The copywriting here is also direct. It tells the buyer exactly what they should do. Put their dreams first by taking advantage of sales and how they'll benefit. And it uses all the right grammatical conventions to drive that action.

It's written in the second person and it uses the present and active tenses. It's also fairly conversational. None of the languages are complex or academic. It reflects how customers actually speak. And finally, the headline is straightforward and it avoids the temptation to be witty or clever. Notice how they've broken the message down into two parts: Weekend sale and put your dreams first today and learn for only 28.99

Canadian. The first part is short, sweet and to the point. The second is longer and more involved, and it's written as a full sentence using a full sentence. Here, let's them write a longer, clearer and ultimately more informative message.

Chapter Summary Questions. Have you defined your feature set linked your features to advantages connected those advantages to your value and benefits and group similar value benefits together? Have you built a messaging framework to be used across your go to market team? And have you zeroed in on your copywriting and messaging to make sure the go to market team is telling the right story in the right way? 17. chapter Summary Exercise - Messaging Have you defined your feature set, linked your features to advantages, connected those advantages to your value and benefits, and grouped similar value / benefits together? Have you built a messaging framework to be used across your go to market team? Have you zeroed in on your copywriting and messaging to make sure the go to market team is telling the right story in the right way?

Messaging Takeaway

The most important thing to remember from this chapter is that you have to make important strategic trade off decisions about what your messaging is and is not going to emphasize.

This involves mapping your features and benefits to what specific decision makers value. It also involves using the foundational tactics of persuasion and marketing psychology.

Go to Market Team Part 1

Part four Go to the market team who needs to get involved? Going to market is a team sport. There might technically be a go to market owner, and in smaller organizations this might even be the CEO. But ultimately it's a collaborative effort. Generally go to market teams are made up of everyone who touches the customer throughout the customer life cycle sales, marketing and customer success or support. This chapter dives into the details of the how of going to market with a special emphasis on the go to market team and their various roles and responsibilities.

This chapter is divided into three chapters, each focusing on a particular segment of the go to market team. We focus on explaining the role of marketing, product, marketing and demand gen. Sales in high and low ACV settings and customer success Marketing. Marketing often leads the go to market strategy because they have so much influence early on. As you might have noticed, marketing covers most of the stages of go to market strategy that we've covered so far. Marketing teams are also well positioned to lead the go to market strategy because they connect product sales and customer success. When it comes to going to market, marketing's role is divided into two large branches. The first is product marketing. Product marketing's role is to do everything we've outlined so far.

Define the audience, identify the market, define the value proposition, create the messaging, and outline the channel mix.

Oftentimes product marketing is heavily involved in both internal and customer facing content, including research papers, blog posts and webinars, battle cards, sales wikis and persona documents and case studies. The second is demand generation. The role of demand generation is to further define the channel mix, execute the actual marketing campaigns, and I iterate and test to drive down the cost of acquiring customers. Each of these functions can also cover additional areas of expertise, including field marketing, brand marketing, content marketing and digital marketing. In smaller organizations, these functions are often all run by 1 or 2 people with product marketing taking on content and brand and demand gen taking on digital and field marketing.

Sales. Sales is responsible, for one thing, closing business. This function is so critical that most organizations go to extreme lengths to keep their sales team motivated and laser focused on that and only that. How you approach sales with your go to market team depends on your average contract value or ACV. Why? Because sales means headcount. The most expensive part of any go to market strategy. That means that you need to be selling something that's valuable enough to justify a salesperson and their salary, plus make the commission worth their time. For instance, say you're selling cell phone cases online for 3.99 each. That value isn't high enough to justify a sales team. Conversely, if you're selling construction equipment for $10 million, then it's definitely worth the sales salary.

Generally speaking, B2B sales is worth having that high touch 1 to 1 sales experience because the ACV tends to be higher. On the other hand, B2C gravitates towards low touch, transactional hands off sales. High SUV sales. B2B high ACV sales teams going to market are structured like this. Market development reps are responsible for responding to inbound leads. These teams increasingly report into marketing rather than sales. Business development reps are responsible for outbound prospecting and booking meetings for account executives to close business. Account executives are responsible for handling the meetings that inbound and outbound reps book and taking customers from an initial meeting to a close deal. Account executives might be field reps on the road and visiting customers in person or part of an inside sales team.

When you're building your go to market strategy, you need to carefully consider how many reps you're going to need and in what roles to achieve your specific business goals. This goes for large and small organizations because at a small one or a startup, you're deciding how many bodies to hire. And at large ones you're deciding how many bodies to dedicate to the product. In both cases, you're committing significant resources, which means that you need to think carefully about how you're going to achieve a positive ROI. Sales Operations. There's one more critical sales function that you need to go to market sales operations. For any business, the key to successful go to market execution is twofold. One, finding opportunity for growth in your organization's data or the market if you're a startup. And two, understanding and adapting your tactics and strategy on the fly in response to early indicators you see in sales data as it rolls in.

For instance, say you're selling bulldozers to mid-sized manufacturing firms. Your sales cycles might be 12 months long, but you don't want to find out a year down the line to find out your positioning is all wrong or your messaging isn't resonating. You need to be tracking data along the way to optimize your conversion rate at every step of the sales cycle. And because sales teams are the bleeding edge of customer interactions, they're the ones that actually gather the data that other departments use to make decisions. Which means you need a clear sales process before you go to market so that you can track performance over time and see if your go to market initiative is on track to achieve your overall goal. It's often worth hiring or getting a freelancer to help you set up your go to market sales process and make sure you're capturing the data you need as prospects go through the buying process.

Low ACV sales. B2C. Sales teams usually play a much smaller role in B2C organizations or B2B organizations selling to small businesses because the average contract value is low. Instead, the final point to point sale is executed through a different transactional mechanism. This can be through a channel distribution partner. For example, if your product is stocked in a store or sold on Amazon through an e-commerce store that you control or in your own store.

Go to Market Team Part 2

Customer success. The final major component of the go to market team is customer success. This is the team that guides customers from when they sign a contract. Through implementation and on to continuing success for software as a service businesses who rely on customers renewing to achieve profitability. Customer success is critical because they're responsible for keeping the customers that close sales in addition to their implementation and support responsibilities. Customer success is increasingly responsible for renewals, upsells and cross-sells, primarily because upsells and cross-sells are fantastic for a business. Upsells and Cross-sells Ingrain your company into the lives of your customers.

Decreasing customer churn and increasing the customer value as they purchase more products. Most importantly, though, you've already spent a big chunk of time and resources to acquire them. The more value you can extract from them, the better your return on investment. And if you include customer success on the go to market team, then you can strategically acquire customers who will grow into high value accounts over time. Customer success can drive profitability because. Number one. Word of mouth only happens if you have happy customers. And since word of mouth has proven again and again to be the most cost effective marketing channel, ignoring it is literally leaving money on the table.

Word of mouth is especially important if you are a small or unknown brand or startup. When every customer is critical to your overall success. Number two, customer acquisition costs are too high to not retain her subscription freemium and try before you buy products. In particular, retention is critical to the economics of your organization. You need to keep your churn rate low. But even for companies selling one-off products, it's far less expensive to keep a customer than to acquire a new one. Upsells and Cross-sells rely on happy customers. You're not going to buy more of something if the organization you purchased from sucks in order to drive high margin cross-sell and upsells, which is high margins. Since you've already paid to acquire the customer, you need to have happy customers, which means investing significantly in support and customer success.

Churn and retention. One of the core metrics for customer success is churn, especially for subscription services that rely on customer retention to grow. Churn rate can be calculated two ways. Revenue churn is the percent of your revenue you've kept over a specific time period. For example, if you had $100,000 of monthly recurring revenue or MMR in January and $80,000 of MMR in February, your churn rate would be the product of subtracting $100,000 from $80,000. And dividing that by $100,000. Basically, 20% of your monthly recurring revenue from last month isn't going to recur this month since it left. You can do the same calculation on an annual basis for annual recurring revenue or RR. The second kind of churn is customer churn or loco churn. This is the same calculation, but instead of taking the revenue value, you count the number of customers.

So if we go back to our example from earlier, that $100,000 in revenue might be 100 customers and ten customers left, your logo churn would be 10%. Churn is important to know because every dollar you churn out is a dollar of new business you need to go and find. If your churn gets too high, it becomes incredibly difficult to grow. You can also use churn to help with your segmentation. Here's an example In segment A, you have a churn rate which is unsubscribes per month of 3%. And in Segment B, your churn rate is 6%. Here you can see that segment B has a higher churn rate with 6% of subscribers abandoning the service each month. It could be that segment B is just not an ideal customer target group. Or it could be that you need to make some tweaks to keep them happy and keep them coming back.

Data can't really tell you what to do. It needs to be interpreted in the context of your overall company vision to decide which action to take. The solution here is not obvious at all. All we know is that Group B is more likely to unsubscribe than is Group A. Customer Lifetime value. LTV. Closely related to churn is customer lifetime value or LTV. Customer lifetime value is a measure of how valuable a customer is to your company. It's actually somewhat complicated to calculate. So I'm going to start with a simplified approach. Year one profit is $1. Year two profit is $2. Year three profit is $2. Year four profit is $0. This table shows the profit coming from a particular customer in each year since he became a customer. You can see that he stopped becoming a customer in year four, hence the $0 in profit. So the lifetime of the customer is three years. The lifetime value can be calculated by adding up the profit for those three years. $1 plus $2 plus $2 equals $5. The customer lifetime value is thus $5. This is a simple formula. A more sophisticated method touches on the world of finance. This more elaborate formula accounts for churn rates, the cost of customer acquisition, and something called the discount rate.

Let me explain. In years two and three, you can see that profit was $2. But because of the time value of money, money today is worth more than money tomorrow. So that $2 in year two is actually worth more than $2 in year three. That's because $2 in year two could have been invested in appreciated for an entire year. But there are other factors here besides the time of value. There's also risk and uncertainty associated with future profits that don't apply to the present. Lifetime value is easier to calculate if your company relies heavily on customer relationship management, software or CRM. If your company doesn't use CRM, then you may need to estimate lifetime value based on sampling customers through market research. What you may discover is that some of your customers are actually losing you money. You should try your best as a marketer to avoid these types of customers.

If they abandon you, do not send them discounts or offers to return. Try to focus your communications on the most profitable segments. Closely connected to lifetime value were these other metrics. ARPU average revenue per user. Be careful with this metric because averages can be deceiving. Often the bulk of your revenue comes from a tiny group of people. In that case, an average would be a misleading figure. ARPU average revenue per paying user in some markets such as free to play gaming, the bulk of people may pay nothing. That's why the average revenue per paying user may be more meaningful. The reason we're talking about these metrics here is that they're incredibly important for customer success.

At the very least, customer success as part of the go to market team has the responsibility of reducing or eliminating churn. Increasingly, they're also responsible for growing accounts, increasing ARPU, ARPU and LTV. If you're relying heavily on expansion to reach your goals, you need to watch these metrics like a hawk. Assembling your team for a B2B business to deliver a cohesive go to market strategy. They need to have marketing, sales and customer success in place. Marketing is needed to identify the market opportunity that the go to market team is going to exploit. Basically, they answer the question Where are we going to market and with what? For the most part, the task of answering this question is owned by product marketing. But marketing is also needed to inform and convince people to buy in a low HCV environment or talk sales in a high HCV environment. This task is owned by demand generation.

Sales is needed to turn leads into closed business. Essentially, sales is responsible for actually taking the product or service and getting it into the hands of customers. And customer success is needed to delight customers so they stick around for a long time. Customer success also needs to keep customers happy so that they can upsell more of the same or cross sell additional products while also telling the world how great you are. Once these three parts are in place, you have what Jim Collins in his book Good to Great has called the flywheel. Essentially, marketing acquires customers' sales, closes them, and customer success delights them, which in turn drives acquisition, sales and delight.

Onwards and onwards as you take over your chosen marketplace. Chapter Summary Questions. Have you assembled your complete go to market team, including marketing, sales and customer success? Our clear roles, expectations and SLAs defined across the go to market team. Have you calculated LTV and churn and linked both figures back to your overall business goal? So you know the benchmark values for both. 21. Summary Exercise - Go-to-Market Team Have you assembled your complete go to market team, including marketing, sales, and customer success? Are clear roles, expectations, and SLAs defined across the go to market team? Have you calculated LTV and churn and linked both figures back to your overall business goal so you know the benchmark values for both?

Go-to-Market Team Takeaway

The main thing to remember from this chapter is that go to market success is fundamentally cross-functional. That means you need to empower the sales team, the product team and the customer success managers.

It also means you need to take responsibility for things you don't necessarily have control over. That requires political skills to get buy-in and execution from other departments.

Demand Generation Part 1

Part five Demand Generation. How to Build Demand for Your Product. Demand generation is all about getting the right people to put up their hands and say, I'd like to talk to a sales person about your product or service. Essentially, it's the place to go to market.

Demand generation is especially critical in the B2B world where every deal is worth more and you can therefore spend a lot more money acquiring each customer. And buying is a long, drawn out and collaborative process involving lots of moving parts and different people. This chapter will cover the demand generation process, theory and stages. Walk through an example Demand generation campaign. Identify the most common demand gen tactics and demonstrate a full demand gen channel mix. The demand generation process is moving from someone who doesn't know who you are to the point they're ready to evaluate your solution. If you think of this conceptually, it looks like a funnel. I am looking at a graphic that demonstrates the funnel. At the top of the funnel is awareness with an arrow pointing down. There's an arrow to the side of awareness that indicates brand awareness.

First time visitors generate interest and education in the middle of the funnel is considered with an arrow pointing down the arrow to the side indicating evaluation of brand and products and speaking directly to customers. And the bottom of the funnel is conversion with an arrow pointing down and the arrow to the side indicates product descriptions, value propositions and transactions. And it says reference Semrush. Awareness. Awareness is the stage when customers don't know who you are or what you do. They need to be educated and made aware of your brand. The goal here is to be helpful. Help them learn things that are interesting. Help them solve a problem they have, even if they don't use your tool to do it.

Common tactics and channels here include blogging and SEO and brand channel awareness campaigns where the focus is simply to get your name in front of Target customers. Out-of-home campaigns, TV ads, influencer marketing and impression based social media ads can all play in this arena. Consideration. Consideration is when they're looking at different vendors and are considering you as a potential solution. They know who you are. They know the problem they need to solve, and they're considering if you can do it. The goal here will depend a lot on your sales process. For some businesses, this is when you put them in touch with a sales team. For other organizations, this is when you continue to promote content, but content that requires a bigger time commitment from your prospects. For example, webinars, white papers, and recorded demos.

Evaluation, evaluation and conversion is when prospective customers are looking at your specific solution and are evaluating you in a lot more detail. This is when you're best positioned to talk about yourself. If it's a transactional business, this is when the purchase happens. Key assets include product and pricing pages, free trials and e-commerce purchasing. For larger, more complex products, prospects at this stage are typically handed off and enter the sales cycle. Alternative

Model. Another framework for modeling the customer decision journey is presented below from McKinsey and Company. I'm looking at a graphic that has two circles on either side. The circle on the left side says Initial consideration set and there's an orange arrow curving over to the other circle.

The arrow is labeled active evaluation, information gathering and shopping. And the circle on the right side is labeled moment of purchase. There's another orange arrow curving towards the initial consideration set and that arrow is labeled post purchase experience and ongoing exposure. There's a star under the initial consideration set that's labeled trigger. And there's another arrow called loyalty loop that is curving back to the moment of purchase. And the text at the bottom reads Here you can see the importance of trigger events that start the buying process. This might include events such as changing account software, expanding to a new store, getting a divorce or moving. Demand generation does not equal lead generation. One of the biggest problems with demand generation is that everybody talks about how they need more leads, but no one knows what a lead actually is. I don't even like to use the word leads because there are too many vastly different types.

Here's a proven process with various types of leads. Awareness. MCL marketing captured lead. These may be cold leads acquired from a purchase list or compiled by your team. Emil equals marketing engaged lead. These are leads that have some soft engagement with you, such as filling out a form to acquire a white paper or webinar or visiting a booth at a trade show. Consideration MQL equals marketing qualified lead. These are usually leads that have responded to a high bar offer, such as a demo consultation or price quote. Sometimes they are just leads that accumulated enough lead scoring points that they are handed to sales even if they haven't actually requested an offer that would in and of itself qualify them to speak to sales.

Evaluation. Sal equals sales accepted lead. These are leads that have been handed to sales that are accepted rather than rejected and are being followed up by sales. SQL equals sales qualified lead. These are leads that engage with sales. SCO equals sales qualified opportunity. These are leads that are candidates for buying your products within a reasonable time frame and have potential revenue pipeline associated with them. The non linear demand process. Demand generation has received a lot of flack in recent years, primarily because the above model rarely reflects how a person discovers a product and decides to buy from them. For instance, say you're selling B2B software.

Someone might not be aware of your product, but see your listing on a review website. They jump immediately to consideration. Likewise, intent channels like Google ads means that leads can enter your funnel at any stage. While this has always been the case, after all, a sales rep can always call someone who says, Actually, yes, I'm evaluating solutions right now. It now happens a lot more often. The funnel is still worthwhile. And if you're tracking efficiently, you can use it to see where you need to refine your go to market strategy. Remember, your funnel doesn't represent the journey every lead takes to become a customer.

Demand Generation Part 2

Demand gen campaign example. Let's put what we just covered into practice. Here's how a demand gen campaign might unfold. Step one: Buy a list of prospects. Once you know what kind of customers you want, you can go and buy a list of 10,000 or 20,000 people who fit your target. There are lots of list brokers and suppliers out there, but try to find someone who can give you the most specialized list for your market. Also, consider testing a few sample lists from different suppliers. I've had a lot of difficulty with suppliers providing very poor quality lists and being very late with deliveries. So the earlier you can get on top of this, the better.

It's worth thinking about how you want to filter your list as well. For B2C products, demographics are almost always the starting point. For example, men 25 to 35 years old who make over $75,000 a year for B2B companies. The starting point is usually firmographics, followed by job titles. But those are only to start. There are infinite ways to slice and dice your prospects to get the customer you want. For B to C, you might segment by location previous purchases, interests, habits, brands they follow, or social platform activity. For B2B, you might segment by company growth department growth, number of locations, what technology they currently use, team size or company age.

The point is the finer you can tune your filters when you're purchasing contacts to manage your ideal customer, the better off you're going to be. Note it's best to write a white paper that aligns well with the problem your product solves or the aspiration your product helps make a reality. Step two: write a white paper. This should be something educational that addresses the pain or aspiration of your target customers. For example, ten Tips for Generating $5 Million Selling Clothing Online. You can create the white paper in a Google slide and simply export as a PDF. You could also create it in a Google Doc InDesign or any number of programs. Step three: Advertise the white paper on Facebook and LinkedIn.

Prospects should have to enter, at the very least, their email address in order to get access to the white paper. The reason we are advertising the white paper is because it's a good top of the funnel offer. Other offers such as requested demo or get a consultation or bottom of funnel offers that don't perform well when promoted to cold leads. Remember you are advertising the white paper, not your company and not your product. An important concept in demand generation is that you want to promote the offer itself and the benefits of the offer rather than your company or product. In this case, the offer is the white paper. Step four: Promote the White paper through content syndication. Promote your white paper far and wide using content syndication. You could, for example, pay the firm pure B2B for each white paper download.

Not only will they promote your paper to your target customers, but they'll also identify the subset of people who are ready to buy. Step five: Nurture the people who download the White Paper. Add the people who download your white paper into an email sequence in a program such as outreach, for example, email number one. I saw you downloaded the white paper title name, so I thought you might like this chapter on topic. Name email too. Here are a few tips to achieve X Email three. Here's a chapter of someone who achieved what you want to achieve. Email for I can teach you how to achieve X. Are you interested in learning more? Email five. I can show you the fastest, simplest way to make this pain go away. Book a demo with me and I'll show you how. At the end of this campaign, you should have generated some marketing qualified leads that sales can convert into opportunities and then into one deal. The key is to evaluate the total cost for the number and value of opportunities created, then revenue generated. Then decide two things. One. Was the ROI on this campaign? Positive.

Basically, did you get more money out than you put in? To. Was this the best use of marketing dollars? This question often goes unasked, but every single dollar spent on marketing has an opportunity cost of a campaign you didn't run. Therefore, even if a campaign has a positive ROI, there might have been a better allocation of resources. Seven Common demand gen tactics. Now that we have an idea of the basics of demand. Gen, let's look at the most common tactics you would like to use as you launch your new product.

It's relatively easy even for a small team to use all these tactics. And as we'll see when we turn our attention to the marketing mix, using multiple tactics is usually the most effective campaign strategy. One. Acquire leads or customers through Google and Bing ads. Google and Bing ads are particularly effective at acquiring leads quickly because their intent focused channels. That is, you can bid on keywords that people are searching for when they have the intent to purchase. The disadvantage is that in the long run, pay per click ads aren't as cost effective as other tactics, such as content marketing. That's because the payoff from pay per click ads is generally linear, as indicated by the term pay per click. In contrast, content marketing, PR and branding generate economies of scale over time.

Another key advantage of search ads is that they can target people at the bottom of the funnel. For example, those who have a high purchase intent and are willing to talk to a sales person. You do this by targeting specific keywords tied to your solution, such as how do I integrate X with Y best software for x or buy x? What this means is that search engine advertising can quickly move the needle on pipeline and sales in ways that other marketing, such as white papers, cannot. One of the main keys to success is having dedicated PPC landing pages. You generally do not want to direct PPC traffic to your home page. One of the main keys to success is having dedicated PPC landing pages. You generally do not want to direct PPC traffic to your home page. You want to create a page that compels people to fill out a form or in some cases to buy your product. For example, you might ask people to book a demo and provide a lot of social proof as to why you are the best, such as ratings from third parties and testimonials.

To acquire leads through Facebook and LinkedIn ads. Facebook and LinkedIn offer incredibly detailed demographic and firmographic targeting data so you can serve focused ads to your specific buyer personas. The challenge, though, is that Facebook and LinkedIn ads don't reflect intent. You can target the exact people who usually buy your product, but not the people who are looking to buy your product right now. So leads generated from Facebook and LinkedIn should generally be connected to a lead nurturing program, such as a series of emails you send out via a sales engagement outreach or salesloft or an email automation system such as HubSpot or Pardot. Intent versus behavior. Example I worked at a B2B SaaS startup called Upchain. We used both Facebook and Google ads to drive leads.

We first started with Google bidding on keywords relevant to our product with a call to action book demo. It was going great, so we decided to roll out Facebook ads, too. We directed them to the same high converting landing page, but our conversion rate plummeted. Why? Because our Facebook audience wasn't ready for a demo. They had no intent to purchase now, but they were the right people to purchase eventually. So we changed our approach. We switched our CTA on Facebook to a whitepaper, all about how to build and scale the manufacturing tech stack. A problem we solved really effectively. Then we nurtured these leads over time with content focused email marketing. Eventually by tailoring our CTA to match the stage of the buyer's journey our audience was in. Facebook became one of our most effective channels. The leads just took longer since we had to wait for them to be ready to buy. Three. Event Marketing. Event marketing is essentially going to events in order to meet your prospects in person. Event marketing usually has a handful of different goals. Getting your product in front of prospects, turning meetings with your prospects into close business and meeting with existing deals to accelerate sales velocity.

Event marketing continues to be a leading channel for B2B demand gen marketers. A 2018 study by Demand Gen Report found that events were the number one most successful tactic for accelerating mid and late funnel leads and the number three tactic for engaging early funnel leads. On top of the revenue generation objectives, there are significant brand awareness benefits that come from events. There are few other ways to get your brand in front of as many as your ideal client profile than at a trade show or conference. For the simple reason they're all in the same place at the same time. Go to the market. Teams should use events wisely, though. For example, sponsoring an event usually requires a significant minimum bid, so dipping a toe in testing isn't an option. What's more, events fall under the lightning strike model of marketing, spending a lot of cash all in one place to make a big impact. That means from a marketing perspective, events can be a risky mood. That's especially true if you're new to event marketing. But don't let this deter you.

If your industry has a single powerful event that you can hitch onto, then it might be a good place to launch your new product or solution. Alternatively, events can form part of your channel mix to build awareness at the top of the funnel. Take meetings in the middle and accelerate deals to close at the bottom. How to get the most from events. Step one: Choose your events carefully. Events represent a huge investment for a company, so you need to pick which events you attend carefully. This should essentially be an exercise similar to target customer work we discussed earlier. Get your audience breakdown from every major event you're considering. See what percentage of attendees are likely to fit your target audience.

Use these to calculate a rough estimate of how many potential high quality leads there are at the event, and apply your historical or projected conversion rates to calculate a projected ROI. Here's an example of this work. Assuming a 20% MQL sal conversion rate and a 30% close rate. Total number of attendees. 5000. Percent of attendees who fit your ICP. 15. Number of potential leads. 750. Number of Mqls. You can expect 150. Number of closed deals you can expect is 75. If you do this for every event, you'll get a sense of how much return you can expect for your investment.

Looking at potential Mqls also gives you a good barometer to compare each event to other non-event marketing channels. Step two: Define a goal for each event. Just like any other channel, events can be used to achieve different objectives: brand awareness, new opportunity creation or existing pipeline acceleration. You need to define a goal for every event so you understand how to measure success as well as what level you need to pull. Depending on where your go to market strategy is lagging.

Demand Generation Part 3

Brand awareness versus events ROI. I used to work at a software startup when I joined. Events were a big part of their marketing mix, representing the lion's share of marketing spend. However, when I dug into where opportunities and deals were coming from, it was never from events. It looked to me like we were spending big money on events and not seeing a return on that spend. But every time I tried to challenge the story that events are good, I was met with resistance.

Turns out it was with good reason. Because every time we went to an event, even if the event didn't pay for itself, the impact on our brand awareness was huge. We'd get people coming up to us and saying, You guys are everywhere. By spending big at events, we were able to create the illusion of size and drive significant brand awareness among our ICP. The result was that we were constantly being brought into deals against our competitors who had raised hundreds of millions of dollars with outbound sales teams of 50 to 100 reps. For content marketing and SEO. Content marketing is all about creating content, videos, webinars, blog posts, white papers, ebooks, etcetera that your target audience finds helpful or interesting. The goal is to provide value so you can create the space to talk about your product or service.

Provide value and build brand equity in your target audience so that when they are looking, they know who to go to. More tactically, content marketing does two things. First, it creates content that people are willing to use their contact information, usually an email address to gain access to. Once you have that contact information, you can market to them to see if they need your product or service. The white paper used earlier in our demand generation campaign is a good example of this. Second, by creating online content like blog posts. Content Marketing Boosts your website's position in Google Search Results.

This means that when your target audience goes looking for answers to their problems, your website is more likely to show up in the search results and they'll be more likely to click on your link. Once they do that, you have the opportunity to convert them into marketing. Captured leads Mqls. The second task is tied closely to search engine optimization or SEO. SEO is the art of understanding what people are searching for and creating the content and response to those search queries. It's also the science of getting your content to rank higher than everyone else. There are dozens of guides to SEO Ahrefs, Brian Deane and Moz SEO all have excellent resources, so we're not going to get too granular here. But from a go to market perspective, there are a few things to call out.

Content marketing and SEO takes a long time. While other channels like search engines or social media marketing can be quickly turned on and off, content takes a long time to generate and SEO takes a long time to work. Content marketing and SEO has lower acquisition costs in the long run. Not only do leads from organic search tend to convert at a higher rate, but they also cost less. Paid acquisition is a linear cost model. You need to spend more to get more up to a certain point where spending more doesn't get you more. For content and SEO, though, the initial cost of generating a piece of content can pay dividends for months or years. And because virtually the entire cost is up front for every new lead that's acquired, your customer acquisition cost drops for that channel. Over time. This makes content marketing and SEO one of the most cost effective marketing channels today.

Keep your content customer centric. It can be tempting to create content from your perspective rather than from the perspective of your customers. For instance, it's fairly easy to break your content up into chapters based on key product features. But this isn't usually how customers think. They don't spend every day obsessing over your product and its capabilities. Instead, they are spending their time worrying about things like how to grow their business, speed up their process, or stop customers from leaving. So it is a good idea to organize your content from the top down, beginning with customer pain points and aspirations.

Once you have covered those, you can introduce information about product features that show that you can address each pain, point and aspiration. For example, a title on your page might say Reduce inventory carrying costs. Beneath this, you can talk about product features that help customers reduce inventory carrying costs, such as with our proprietary forecasting algorithm, you'll cut waste production by 33% on your website. It can be very helpful to have specific chapters for each major customer group. This forces you to write content in a customer centric way rather than listing product details in an egocentric way.

Content Examples. Webinars. Webinars, especially ones that provide educational content, are one of the most effective ways to acquire customers. There are great ways for you to offer educational value to prospective customers, and they're a good medium for providing technical information about your product or service. Because of that, they can effectively pull those prospects still in the consideration phase out of the woodwork and they can help you to accelerate deals already in motion. You can promote your webinar using your email database of leads. Don't be afraid to be aggressive here. You can send out multiple emails to get as many people to register as possible, and you should also be sure to send multiple reminder emails to ensure that people who register actually attend the event.

Once the webinar is over, send out the recording and encourage people to call or email to get more information. There are a few things you can do to keep your audience engaged. One Put polls or questions into the content to try and build a rapport and get as much back and forth as possible. Three. Add in a survey at the end to gather market intelligence to hone your marketing. Four Keep it short. 30 minutes is best, but 45 if you really need more time. Case studies. According to research in Harvard Business Review, the case study is the single most read piece of content that companies produce. Humans are social animals. We are natural conformists who rely on social proof to validate our own behavior. And this makes case studies extraordinarily powerful pieces of content marketing. They show that someone similar to your prospective customer has achieved success using your product or service. Case studies are particularly effective if you can quantify results.

Quantitative data helps your prospects to understand the source of value, and it gives them a very tangible, specific aspiration. Case studies are also effective because they can be used to tell a compelling story about your product or service. According to the copywriter Bob Lai case studies should be written like journalistic articles instead of producing a dry analysis. Tell an exciting story about how one customer achieved all that they ever dreamed of because of your product. To make the most out of your case. Studies try to get as much content as possible. Bring a videographer with you to interview the client in person and make a video case study. Edit down the best bit to a 92nd video. Get the best snippets for 10 to 15 Second social media video ads. Turn the interview into a customer story page on your website.

Build a downloadable PDF case study that's longer and more detailed. Run a webinar where you interview the client on what's been successful. Viral content. A lot of marketers scoff at the idea of creating viral content as part of a go to market strategy. They don't take viral planning seriously. We do. We take it seriously because the research on different customer journeys suggest word of mouth is the single most important factor. People hear about products from other people. So one way or another, a good marketer will need to find a way to drive word of mouth. The second reason we take virality seriously is because one of the top business schools in the world does. There is some serious research on viral marketing that's happened at Wharton, the Ivy League business School at the University of Pennsylvania.

Our foundation for viral marketing comes from Wharton professor Jonah Berger, author of the book Contagious. Here's the framework for creating viral content called the Steps Framework. Each letter represents a factor in virality. I'll walk you through each of these. Social currency. People like to share things that make them look good to others. For example, you might share a company's video if it makes you look intelligent. Triggers. People share things when they are triggered to do so with reminders. For example, Irish products are likely to get shared on Saint Patrick's Day. Emotion.

People share things that are emotionally arousing. Content that makes us angry or uplifted is likely to energize us to take action and share it. Public. When something is public, it is far more likely to spread than. Something that is private. For example, an Apple laptop with a visible logo is more likely to spread than a laptop with no logo on it. Practical value. Things that provide practical, useful information are likely to get shared. For example, a tip sheet on buying a new home will likely get shared with a friend who is looking to buy a new home. Stories. People tend to think more in terms of narratives than in terms of facts. Embedding a brand message in a story with a beginning, middle and end is more likely to be remembered and shared than a list of benefits. Five.

Email marketing. Despite persistent claims that email is dead, it continues to be an incredibly effective demand generation tactic for both B2B and B2C channels. It's cost effective and fast to deploy, and it can play a strong supporting role for other demand gen tactics like content marketing. The basic idea of email marketing is to send out emails to your target audience automatically and over a long period of time called a drip campaign to keep your brand top of mind, educate them on the problem you solve and try to get them to convert a lead or a customer with compelling offers or calls to action.

There are four common drip campaigns that apply to both B2B and B2C companies. Which campaign style you choose will depend on the resources, sophistication and tech stack that you have access to. That said, remember, there's no silver bullet in marketing. And this goes for email marketing as well. If you have the capacity, try multiple strategies and compare results at the end.

Demand Generation Part 4

Email newsletter Drip campaign. This is by far the easiest campaign to build and deploy. An email newsletter usually consists of a few content pieces that you've produced, some industry relevant news and perhaps some news about your business. If you're a B2C company, the newsletter is usually an opportunity to show what new products or updates you have and a chance to offer some kind of discount. Email newsletters usually go out to the entire user base, and you can streamline this process by using a tool like MailChimp.

Audience based drip campaign. Audience based drip campaigns are email campaigns that segment your target audience by who they are. For example, say you're a B2B business who sells a complex product with lots of buyers involved in the process. You might separate out your buying committee into different personas, then serve them different content based on who they are and what your value proposition means to them. From a B2C perspective, this would be similar to segmenting based on demographic information. For example, an e-commerce clothing company serving women's clothes to women and men's clothes to men.

Since audience specifics are usually fairly fixed, this can be executed with simple software like MailChimp. Content based drip campaigns. Content based drip campaigns are designed so that you have multiple drip campaigns, each one focusing on content from a different product value or theme. Users are added to a top level content mixer campaign, which has content from every subgroup. When a user responds to one of the master mixer emails, they're redirected so that they then get served more content like the content they engaged with. Content based drips are more complicated than audience and newsletters for the simple reason that who gets what email and what you're basing that on changes over time. But they tend to have better engagement because you're basing each new email on what worked effectively before.

Since content based drips are complex to execute, you'll usually need to use tools like HubSpot, Pardot, Marketo or Eloqua. Intent based drip campaigns. The last type of drip campaign is intent based drip campaigns. Here, each new email that you send to a specific prospect is based on their previous engagement with your business. This engagement might be a website visit, previous email opens or clicks clicking on an ad or reading, watching, consuming, or downloading your content. In the B2C world, intent based campaigns work well. If you can retarget users based on the products they were looking at and didn't purchase.

In the B2B world, intent based campaigns can form a crucial part of your lead qualification process by serving content that is relevant to the particular point that the prospect is at in their decision process. Operationally, this is usually done with lead scoring. Users with a low score might be served content focused on educating them about the problem you solve. Those with higher scores might get emails that focus on quantifying the value of your solution, for example, with an ROI calculator. Don't let perfect be the enemy of good. Marketers often get analysis paralysis when they try to figure out how best to maximize their email efforts. I always chuckle when I hear people talk about the perfect time to send an email.

The common wisdom is that Tuesday morning is somehow the optimal time to send out business emails. But I have also seen research suggesting that click through rates are particularly high on weekends, even though open rates tend to be lower. People have an odd fixation with the science of email timing, and they buy into the myth that there's a perfect time to get their email out the door. But a controversial opinion. I don't think it's all that important when you send your emails. The timing of your email send should be trumped by the actual value that your emails provide. Deciding whether to mention pain Point A or B in your email is far more important than whether you send it at 11 a.m. Pacific or 11 a.m. Eastern time. Marketers also spend a lot of time worrying about perfecting the graphics in an email. But I've seen research from HubSpot that suggests that plain text emails actually perform better than graphic emails, even though they take a tiny fraction of the time to produce. I've also seen basic emails produced in outreach perform well, even though they don't have graphics at all.

Customers often view basic emails as though they were coming from a friend. Whereas overly slick emails can have an aura of salesmanship that turns customers off. The bottom line, obsessing over design often isn't worth the effort. It is very unlikely that your marketing is going to be so efficient that the extra dollars you gain from optimizing your email, spend time or your graphics will be worth the time it takes to do that. You're much better off spending time making your value proposition stronger or tightening your audience segmentation. So don't let the perfect be the enemy of the good. And don't let the small details trump the big picture of your overall marketing strategy. Six display ads.

Display ads are things like banner ads, YouTube pre-roll ads and text ads that appear on websites other than your own. Depending on which ad network you choose, these can be priced per click. For example, PPC per 1000 impressions or CPM. Generally display ads are only effective as a brand awareness tactic. That's because their click through rate is far lower than channels like Facebook or LinkedIn, but they're often very inexpensive to run and they allow you to retarget users from your website or email campaigns. For your target audience. This can create the impression that your brand is everywhere, as if you launched a big, expensive brand awareness campaign when in reality you are spending pennies per impression. Seven direct mail. That's right. Old school physical direct mail.

Your direct mail could take a few forms. Postcards printed from postcard mania, handwritten notes produced and mailed by services like send. So for a personal touch. Packages that include items like chocolates or merch. Used. Well, direct mail can generate immediate results. For example, you can use direct mail to get a prospect's attention, maybe by offering a free product or trial and then quickly secure a meeting through a follow up email. Direct mail is also effective if your target audience is united by geography. For instance, if you're attending a conference in Texas, you might send direct mail promotions to the people in your CRM who live in Texas.

One example of this comes from when I worked at a large UK based bank and insurance provider. I worked on the marketing team for pet insurance and direct mail was a big part of our marketing mix.

The reason we relied on this is that we were able to identify specific postcodes around the UK that over index for pet owners. That is, if you knocked on 100 doors in that postcode, there was a greater chance of the resident being a pet owner than if you knocked on 100 random doors across the country. This made our direct mail cost effective and thus gave us a good return on investment. Eight. All the others. There are, Of course, lots of other tactics that you can add to your arsenal. These include out of home, traditional media, organic social media, influencer marketing, and more. And if you can layer these into your demand mix and they make financial sense, that's great. But for most go to market plans, the seven tactics listed above will get you most of the way there.

Demand Generation Part 5

Brand versus demand marketing. Brand marketing is often presented as the opposite of demand marketing. In brand marketing, the story goes, measurement doesn't matter. It's all about storytelling and ethereal brand building. In reality, though, brand marketing is a channel like any other. It has metrics and targets. It's just not as easy to link the marketing dollars you spend to the revenue dollars you make.

Brand marketing is primarily focused on making as many positive impressions as possible in order to increase your brand equity. That is the value your brand brings to your organization. A positive brand equity can be extremely powerful. For example, Apple's brand equity is a big part of why they can charge thousands of dollars for an iPhone. Positive brand equity can also act as a form of insurance if your brand is tarnished in any way. Your positive brand equity can help stave off a drop in revenue. Brand marketing is also focused on brand awareness. Generally, brand awareness is a measure of whether people know your brand. But there are different ways to define and measure it. The strongest approach is what's called unaided brand awareness.

This means people can name your brand without any sort of prompts. For example, you might ask a consumer what luxury hybrid cars can you name? They might say Lexus, Lincoln and Cadillac. That's good news for you if you're marketing for Lincoln because you've just proven that at least someone has unaided awareness of your brand. Another popular approach is aided awareness. This is where you, as the market researcher, provide a list of brands or prompts. For example, in a survey you might ask which of the following brands have you heard of? If they check off your brand, then you've demonstrated that they have heard of your brand. This isn't as reliable as unaided awareness, but it's easier to measure and put into surveys. If you're working on big brands, you'll likely get your brand awareness data from a third party such as Nielsen.

Nielsen is one of the leading market research companies and they provide software to track these sorts of KPIs. They regularly conduct research with customers to collect this data. If you're working for a small company, you probably won't have access to this sort of data easily. You may need to send surveys out to random people within your target customer group to help you get a rough estimation of your brand awareness. One of the advantages of doing your own surveys is that you get highly relevant data rather than getting data from the general public. You'll be collecting data with your highly relevant target group of people. You can then measure your brand awareness over time to gauge progress. There are other, more roundabout ways of estimating brand awareness, such as looking at search data for your brand on Google's keyword planner.

Here you can see that Mountain Dew has an average search volume between 100 K and 1 million. Brand A is 30% among yuppies, 11% among deal seekers and 5% among practical buyers. Brand B is 2% with yuppies, 11% with deal seekers and 12% with practical buyers. Brand C is 3% with yuppies, 3% with deal seekers and 8% with practical buyers. Brand D is 1% with yuppies, 19% with deal seekers and 3% with practical buyers. Often what we're interested in is brand awareness by each of the brands in the market, including ours and our competitors, and also by each of the major customer groups in the market. Here, you can see that one of our customer segments called Yuppies is very much aware of Brand A but pretty oblivious to the other brands.

If we own Brand A, then we can see a clear advantage here. Brand B is well known in the two other segments. As a marketing strategist, this information is very useful. Brand A could benefit by advertising more to deal seekers. Brand D might benefit by boosting awareness among deal seekers as well. Brand awareness and brand marketing as a rule involve big expensive campaigns and are usually better suited to mature products further along the product life cycle. When brands do and do not matter, I saw an interesting question on Quora recently. A user was wondering if brands become more important the more the product looks like a commodity. It's an interesting question and we can use it as a jumping off point to demonstrate when and where brands play a significant role in marketing. And maybe more importantly, when they really don't.

This is crucial to dig into because I've seen too many companies invest heavily in branding that doesn't really yield any results. This chapter will help you to determine whether branding should be a priority in your go to market strategy. First, let's look at a couple of commodities. Take gravel, for instance here. Branding doesn't really matter. Businesses will buy gravel regardless of what brand name is slapped on it. Now, think about ketchup. Ketchup is a commodity, too, but here branding actually matters quite a bit. So we have two commodities where the role of branding is very different. Now let's consider something that's not a commodity. Take a Rolls Royce, for example. Here, branding is extremely important for driving purchases. Okay, so what's happening here? In order to understand, we need to break this down. The best place to start is with the seven marketing tactics that create value in the market. These are products, brands, services. Prices.

Communications Incentives and distribution. With commodities like gravel. The product itself doesn't really create value. That's because it is indistinguishable from the competitor's products. So if the product isn't creating value, does that mean the brand needs to? In some cases, that is true, but not always. Think back to our gravel example above, where we determined that branding doesn't really matter for selling this basic commodity. So to really unpack how brands create value, we need to go a level deeper. Essentially, there are three ways that brands can create value. One, they create functional value, such as communicating the quality of the product. Two, they create psychological value, such as portraying your identity through clothing labels. Three. Lastly, they create monetary value, such as communicating the price positioning with business to business commodities such as gravel.

The psychological value of the brand doesn't really matter, nor does the functional or monetary value. If you have a product where the brand doesn't create any of these values, pouring time and resources into branding isn't going to be valuable. But with business to consumer commodities such as ketchup or cornflakes, the brand actually does create psychological value.

When the person eats cornflakes, the brand itself has an impact on the eating experience. You may actually enjoy the product more because it was branded in a certain way. The bottom line brands matter more in context where they can create functional psychological and monetary value. How to build great and creative things. There's no single formula for building great ad creative, but there are three major approaches that you can consider.

When I worked on TV ads, the approach I used and the one I recommend was developed by the acclaimed Leo Burnett advertising agency. It's called The Big Idea. You focus on a single benefit and then highlight attributes that support that benefit. In other words, you communicate one benefit, but you provide prospective customers with multiple reasons to believe in that benefit. The inverse of this is talking about multiple benefits in a single attribute that creates those benefits. For example, automation might lead to lower labor costs, faster processing and reduced wait times. A third approach is storytelling. This one is gaining a lot of traction in the business world today. Humans generally think in terms of narratives, so we can easily recall ads that fit a natural story. With this approach, you typically want to present your product or your offer as the hero of the story.

Many companies will already have a formula for how to do ads, but advanced marketers need to know the right time to use the right approach. To learn more about these approaches and when they're most useful, I'd suggest reading Advertising Strategy by Brian Sternthal and Derek Rucker. But here's a quick and dirty guide. Approach one where you focus on a single benefit is a good approach when you have a single benefit with lots of attributes to support it. For example, Volvo is safe because it has airbags, a collision warning system and a blind spot information system. Approach two Where you focus on multiple benefits is best, where you have a very specific, unique attribute that offers your prospective customers a whole host of benefits. Our automation example applies here.

Again, automation increases speed and accuracy, which in turn saves your customers time, money and other resources. Approach three Storytelling works best when it's important to demonstrate the benefit or benefits. For example, it might work best when it's difficult to convey the value of the product without showing a case study. Storytelling also works well if the product has some kind of emotional or psychological value. Of course, there are other creative strategies that can work in certain situations. For example, if your product has a very strong point of difference, you could simply communicate that buying the product will yield a particular benefit. This aggressive approach can work if the product is unique or if your product is complicated.

Analogies can be much better at communicating value than any other creative approach because they allow you to relate something your prospects don't understand to something with which they're already familiar or comfortable. Chapter Summary Questions. Have you clarified the demand generation process, including definitions and responsibilities with the go to market team? Have you identified your target demand tactics and developed hired or outsourced capabilities in each? Have you identified key tactics for every stage of the demand generation funnel?

Is branding going to be a key part of your marketing strategy? 28. Summary Exercise - Demand Generation Have you clarified the demand generation process, including definitions and responsibilities, with the go to market team? Have you identified your target demand tactics and developed, hired, or outsourced capabilities in each? Have you identified key tactics for every stage of the demand generation funnel? Is branding going to be a key part of your marketing strategy?

Demand Generation Takeaway

The most important thing to remember from this chapter is that successful demand generation requires a holistic view of the entire marketing funnel and the entire customer journey.

You cannot just look at lead generation. You cannot just look at the top or the bottom of the funnel. The vast majority of leads created by marketing departments don't ever convert to revenue because of this myopic perspective. You have to take a holistic view of the funnel across channels and across time.

Product Marketing Fundamentals

Welcome to Product Marketing: Effective Go-To-Market Strategy

The best products can still lose in the marketplace. Why? They are beaten by products with stronger product marketing. Good product marketing is the difference between "also-ran" products versus products that lead. And yet, product marketing is widely misunderstood. Although it includes segmenting customers, positioning your product, creating product collateral, and supporting sales teams, great product marketing achieves much more. It directs the best way to bring your product to market. It shapes what the world thinks about your product and category. It inspires others to tell your product's story.

Product success starts with making the right strategic decisions. But the challenge for many product teams is that they are often so preoccupied with the tactics that they no longer see the forest for the trees.

This Book will help you proactively create a winning product strategy and an actionable product roadmap using a wide range of proven tools and techniques.

So Let's Do This! Enroll now and sharpen your product strategy skills. See you on the inside!

Who this Book is for

1. Product Marketing professionals
2. Product Management professionals
3. Entrepreneurs and small business owners
4. Operations Managers
5. Designers
6. People interested in transitioning to the tech industry

Marketing Mix

Part six The Marketing Mix. How to Measure Channel Effectiveness. Marketing is changing. Historically, we've lived in a supply driven world. That means that supply was low and demand was high. So companies had a lot of power. They focused on the supply chain since the primary concern was getting enough units built and shipped to meet demand.

This is essentially the story of mid-century America. In contrast, we now live in a demand driven world. Consumers hold most of the power, and they can demand that suppliers cater to their specific needs. This is what the Cambridge group refers to as the demand chain as opposed to the supply chain. In this new demand driven world, options have exploded. Needs are specific rather than generic, and the expectation is that those specific needs are met in a specific and targeted way.

On top of these changes, customers do a ton of research on their own, particularly early in the buying stage. This means that B2B marketers need to adapt and meet customers where they are in the buying cycle. The same is true in B2C, where customers turn to reviews to assess products. Because of these changes going to market, teams can no longer afford to rely exclusively on one channel or another. Rather, in an increasingly competitive world, the only way to efficiently go to market is to do so across multiple marketing channels at once and to rely on the aggregate impact being greater than the sum of its parts. So achieving the right marketing mix is a crucial factor in any go to market process.

In this chapter, we're going to do a deep dive into the marketing mix, looking at how to calculate your marketing mix. A Guide to planning out your marketing mix in Excel. And an example of an integrated marketing campaign. Marketers often play favorites advocating one marketing tactic over another. But you can't let your bias get in the way of the growth goals of your business. Here's an example. I am partial to pay per click keyword ads and landing pages.

I particularly like Unbounce because it allows me to quickly create landing pages and test key features such as the header text and the hero image. What is the main image on a web page, landing page or ad? I also love using Google's keyword planner. I was certified in AdWords and I value the timely quantitative data. But in many cases, this type of quantitative, experimental digital marketing isn't the most appropriate approach in professional services marketing, for example, public speaking is arguably the most effective tactic. So marketers need a degree of humility and flexibility with tacks to achieve growth goals.

If I was working in professional services, marketing and constantly pushing pay per click keyword ads over public speaking, I wouldn't be doing my job. But I also wouldn't be doing my job if I only focused on public speaking. Creative and effective marketing mix is generally even more important than identifying the most effective standalone approach. Luckily, there's a process that allows you to remove bias from your tactical decision making. It's called media mix modeling. It uses statistical regressions to identify the ideal mix of different media such as TV, PPC, SEO, et cetera. Here's how it's done.

Calculating the media mix. You can do media mix modeling yourself using Excel, Stata, SPSS or another statistical program. But calculating the optimal media mix can get pretty complicated. Let's start with a simple example. I'm looking at a chart right now with the rows. Say year one, year two, year three. And the columns say sales, TV, print, PPC and SEO. Year one sales are at 20. TV is five. There are two prints. PPC is one. SEO is 0.5. Year two sales are 25. TV is six. There are three prints. PPC is two. SEO is one. Year three sales are 15. TV is two. Print is one. PPC is 0.5 and SEO is 0.2. This table shows a record of sales across three years. It also shows how much was spent on each medium in each year. In year one, 5 million was spent on TV, 2 million was spent on print, 1 million was spent on pay per click advertising or PPC, and half a million was spent on search engine optimization SEO. Here's how you do your media mix marketing with this data.

One click the data tab in Excel and go to data analysis on the far right. If this option isn't available, you need to add the Excel add in for data analysis. Two Select regression from the dropdown and click okay. Three for the Y range. Select the sales column for the X range. Select the columns for TV. Print. ET cetera. Then press. Okay. I'm now looking at a table where the rows say intercept TV, print, PPC and SEO. And the rows are coefficient standard error t stat p value lower 95% upper 95% lower 95.0% and upper 95.0%. And I see two highlighted numbers.

The coefficient for TV is one and the coefficient for PPC is four. This is what your output looks like. Note that PPC has a coefficient of four and TV has a coefficient of one. This tells you that PPC and TV are the best predictor of sales. So if you want to increase sales, you should concentrate your budget here. This was a very basic analysis. As a marketer, you generally rely on your analytics partners to help you develop more sophisticated models. I'm now looking at a graph where there's a blue line that's slowly curving upward and over. That is a red line that starts where the blue line is and slowly curves upward following the same way. But the red line is going higher and there's a red double sided arrow in between both the blue and the red lines.

In this graph I am showing sales on the vertical axis and time on the right axis. In more advanced models, which you would do is establish a base case. My base case here is the blue line. The blue line shows the prediction of sales. If I spent nothing on the media. This would account for existing momentum and seasonality. The red line indicates the predicted sales by spending on media. So you see, what we're really interested in from a management perspective is the space indicated by the Red arrows. This is the real impact of the media. Two issues you may run into when you are analyzing this kind of data. There are two common problems that you might run into. The first is that not all of your data will be quantitative.

For example, male and female are not metrics. In cases like these. First, consider whether those factors are even all that important. Often marketers overemphasize demographic data when in fact motivational or attitudinal data is more important. Second, consider treating the data with dummy variables. For example, zero could mean male and one can mean female. The second issue you might run into is comparing data with different scales. For example, you might have miles, pounds , dollars , inches et cetera. The key to addressing these differences is to standardize the data before you start running statistical analyses that could look something like this. I am looking at two columns.

One column says original data. Under that is one kilometer. Under that is two kilometers. On the right hand column, I see standardized data. Below that is 3.37 and 0.71. Below that average equals 1.5, and standard deviation equals 0.7. This is a simple way to standardize the data. In this example, we have two data points, one kilometer and two kilometers. For each data point, subtract the mean for the data set and then divide by the standard deviation of the data set. Now we have two standardized data points, and we can compare these new standardized data to other data sets that might have pounds dollars inches et cetera.

Marketing Mix Part 2

Building your marketing mix. At this point in the go to market process, you know, your audience, your value proposition and you have a good idea of your marketing demand channels. You know, whether or not a brand is going to be part of your mix. And you've done a ton of work on audience definition, value creation and messaging.

Now it's time to lay it all out in a marketing mix. Your marketing mix is the specific distribution of spend across channels, assets and time. Basically, what money is going, where and when? Triggers versus the funnel. Old school marketers think of the customer decision journey as a linear path, beginning with awareness and ending in purchase. This is the classic funnel and it's served go to market teams for years. But recently, McKinsey developed a more sophisticated framework that suggests that the buying journey isn't linear. Rather, it's actually based on triggers. Triggers are key moments that instigate the buying process.

For example, a company might start researching new software when they reach a certain size and their status quo starts to break down. Or someone might start researching for contract software when they're looking for a new apartment or going through a divorce. These triggers are incredibly important because they are inflection points. They're moments when you can inject your product into the discussion and become highly relevant. With that in mind, you should remember triggers when you're considering your marketing mix. Your mics should aim to one accelerate when those triggers surface for your target customers. To educate prospects about those triggers. Three. Create content that solves the pain. Those triggers have surfaced. And to develop processes and drip campaigns that quickly take prospects from vaguely interested to ready to buy. How to build a marketing calendar.

Building a campaign requires you to work across multiple marketing channels at once, rather than relying on a single marketing tactic to do everything. And in order to do that, you need to develop a way to stay organized and to keep all of your departments on the same page. I've worked on many complex marketing campaigns, including global product launches with multi-million dollar budgets. And I can tell you that when you deal with a lot of different moving parts, you need an ironclad organizational strategy. Otherwise the whole thing goes off the rails fast. Here's how I recommend organizing your marketing mix. One Start with a spreadsheet such as Google Sheets or Microsoft Excel.

Google sheets are generally better because you can collaborate and share it in real time. That way, everyone in your company is on the same page, literally. To make the vertical axis of your spreadsheet the types of marketing assets. So the first column should consist of asset categories. For example, cell two might be videos. Cell three might be printed, and cell four might be banners. Make the horizontal axis time. So your second column might be week one. The third column, week two and so on. It is helpful to also bundle these into months and I'm looking at a chart that has exactly that.

Once you have this framework in place, you can start answering the various marketing items you will use. Here, it's helpful to use color coding. Blue might mean finished. Green might mean released. Note It's important to distinguish between when an item is expected to be finished and when it is actually released to the market. Reserve red for red flag issues such as delays. From here. There are other layers of complexity that you might add. For example, the first tab might relate to product one, whereas another tab might relate to product two. The first half of your sheet might be for one region while the bottom half relates to another.

The bottom line is that you can tweak this general template to the specific needs of your company. Then the only thing left to do is to actually populate your marketing calendar with your channels and assets. Integrated versus Discrete Marketing. The most efficient way to acquire customers is through integrated campaigns, not discrete channel activities. Analytical thinkers like to break things into parts and measure the performance of each of those parts. If Facebook is generating low acquisition costs and LinkedIn isn't, then you would naturally want to pump more money into Facebook. But this approach is overly simplistic.

You have tons of touch points with a customer at various stages in the customer buying cycle. They usually don't decide to buy from you because of one Google ad or because of one social media post. And in situations where that is actually the case, your customer acquisition cost was probably too high. That's because certain channels are more efficient at generating awareness, like banner ads with a very low cost per impression.

Other campaigns are good at generating responses to start the conversation. These are things like Google ads and landing pages. But if you're expecting your Google ads to generate awareness, consideration and purchase, then you're probably being very inefficient. In isolation.

Your data might be telling you that Google ads have the lowest customer acquisition cost. But looking at the bigger picture, you need to think in a more integrated way. By integrating campaigns and structuring each channel and asset to only do what it's good at, you can maximize your marketing spend and your marketing impact without increasing your budget. Lightning strike marketing. Agile approaches to management are very much in vogue right now, and Agile marketing is no exception. The ideas that you test and learn, pivoting as needed based on one the data you acquire through testing, and two how the market reacts to your marketing.

The marketing mix that we just outlined reflects this building channels and testing over time. But there are times when you just need to go big or go home. In the entertainment industry, for example, it often makes more sense to condense your marketing into a very short time frame. That means burning most of your marketing budget right around the time you launch your product. The challenge with entertainment products is that your competition is enormous. Say, for example, that you're marketing a movie. Your competition isn't just other movies. It's not even just other entertainment products like video games or books.

It's all the many substitutes that the market offers. Your prospective customers like spending time with family at the pool or going on a hike or taking a cooking class. So in order to get noticed, you need to put all your resources into a concentrated attack. Entertainment marketing is like launching a rocket ship. You don't fly a few feet in the air each day. Instead, you put all your energy into one giant launch so that you generate enough speed to break through the resistance of the atmosphere. With entertainment marketing, you're trying to break through the noise and clutter in order to capture people's interest and get them into the theater or onto your subscription service.

The safe approach of dipping your toes into the water here and there. Optimizing each step of the way just doesn't generate enough power. With entertainment products such as movies and video games, the lion's share of revenue is generated in the short time just after the product is released to the market. The launch is so critical to success because the revenue curve quickly trails off afterwards. So what does this mean for marketers whose products don't fall into the entertainment category? In most cases, you'll be going to market for the long term, and in that case, you're probably aiming for returns over a long, sustained period of time. But you may still choose to do a lightning strike marketing strategy if you want to jump start your product launch. An integrated campaign example.

Let me walk you through an example of a truly integrated campaign designed to acquire new customers. I'll use a business to business example, but the principles can be applied to B2C as well. Your first step will likely be to buy a list of target companies. This is an important step that many marketers miss. They start running ads, but they haven't actually defined the universe of customers they want to acquire. You can and should narrow down exactly which customers you want to acquire by working with a list broker or a database provider. If you're looking for a general list provider, you can go with a company like Info USA.

If you're looking for a niche database provider, look to a company like EtailInsights. There are also companies like Lithium that will compile lists from scratch. You can test different list providers to figure out which one yields the highest quality. To test your lists, send the exact same email to two lists using a program such as Marketo. Whichever list produces more qualified leads is the winner. Once you've acquired a list of Target customers, your next step is to run and test the lead gen ads. Run lead generation ads precisely to the group of people on your list and no one else. Can you see how efficient this is? Instead of broadcasting to the world, you're broadcasting narrowly to a predefined set of Target customers. Facebook and LinkedIn are two of the most powerful platforms to do this.

They offer lead generation ads that you can use to promote offers such as ebooks, free consultations or free demos. You might be thinking, why would I pay to get someone to download a free ebook? Once again, the answer to this question ties to the point about having an integrated campaign. In isolation. Paying someone to download an ebook would be dumb. But in the context of an integrated campaign, it starts to make a lot of sense. The ad might only generate an e-book download, but the follow up channels might land the actual sale. For example, you might send ten emails to everyone who downloaded the e-book. The seventh email might prompt people to buy from you or at least speak to a sales person.

Folding in direct mail can be valuable here as well. So at this point, you're hitting your prospects with ads and perhaps direct mail. You can also hit them with educational emails that nurture the leads. Typically, these are educational emails that provide value to prospects. You can send these automatically through the market to Infusionsoft, Weber, HubSpot, MailChimp or one of the automation offerings from Salesforce. These are your general marketing emails. You can also use a program like Outreach to solicit prospects with messages from your outbound sales team. These tend to have a more personal one on one tilt to them. While all of this is happening, you could also be running general brand awareness banners on Facebook, LinkedIn and Google.

Retargeting website. Visitors with banner ads can also be effective. The idea here is that you're not relying on a single channel to generate results. You're hitting the same list of prospects with multiple channels, either simultaneously or sequentially. This is an efficient system for acquiring new customers. Chapter Summary Questions. Have you planned out your marketing calendar? Have you secured executive buy in for a mixed channel approach to marketing? Are you pursuing a lightning strike approach to your product launch?

Do you know what your audience triggers are and do you know how to use different channels to deliver the right messages at the right time? 32. chapter Summary Exercise - Marketing Mix Have you planned out your marketing calendar? Have you secured executive buy-in for a mixed-channel approach to marketing? Are you pursuing a lightning strike approach to your product launch? Do you know what your audience triggers are, and do you know how to use different channels to deliver the right message at the right time?

Marketing Mix Takeaway

The main chapter from this chapter is that efficient, scalable marketing involves many moving parts, multiple channels and multiple assets. You should exploit each of these for their unique advantages and organize them all into a central calendar.

Sophisticated marketing is not about attributing individual channels to revenue. It's about integration and holistic execution to achieve economies of scale and synergy.

How Much Pricing Your Product Part 1

Part seven How much is the pricing of your product? Pricing is one of the most challenging elements of the go to market strategy. It's a balance between charging enough to meet revenue expectations and cover costs while being low enough that customers get a positive return on investment for the value you're promising. In this chapter, we're going to cover some of the common pricing strategies, gotchas, and a few tips to maximize your revenue with pricing.

Below this, I see another chart. It's a picture of an excerpt from a textbook. On the left hand side, it says Standardized pricing. And in parentheses it says one product equals one price. And there is a double sided arrow going all the way to the right side that says customize pricing. And in parentheses it says one negotiation equals one price. Below that, it says the pricing tiers. And there are four boxes. The first box says standard price. And it defines price as the same for each client based on product characteristics and market sustainability.

E.g. transaction banking list prices box to say segment pricing. Segment level pricing differentiates price by 2 to 3 relevant variables e.g. rating cross-selling and potential. Box three says client pricing is set at a client level based on several centrally defined factors and using a dedicated pricing tool e.g. industry rating margins, length of relationship churn risk. Box four says negotiated price. Price is set during negotiations with approvals managed centrally, e.g. full rental fees based on ancillary business.

The ultimate pricing model is based on one or more pricing dimensions, product characteristics and target clients reference simon-kucher and partners. This pricing model is designed specifically for software. But most products can find themselves along the axis somewhere. The basic idea behind this diagram is that pricing should have multiple dimensions. These dimensions, which are essentially the variables that impact the price, are usually product dimensions, usage dimensions, volume dimensions and client contract dimensions. It's worth noting that often very simple products will only have one dimension.

For example, when I go and buy a bag of kumquats, I pay a set price. It doesn't matter if I buy 100 bags, which is the volume dimension, or if I'm planning on making a kumquat stew versus a kumquat salad, or how often I shop at the store. Beyond this, the first dimension to be added is almost always product. For example, here's my barber's pricing page. I'm looking at an excerpt from a website from the barber shop Mi Hermano, and it looks like pictures of several services. There's a beard called the Boss Man for $28. Complete beard, shape up and trim with straight razor and hot towel treatment.

Under that is the Torontonian for $38, which is a tailored cut and style. Under that is El Patron, which is $48, which is a tailored cut and style with beard trim and under that is the change up for $48, which is a restyle for medium to long hair. Their pricing list shows that as you spend more, you get more services. For example, if you pay $10 more, you get a beard trim. As products get more complex, however, more dimensions enter the equation. For simple B2C and some SMB focused B2B software, for example, the usual dimensions are product features with usage and contract length, monthly or annually layered on top. Zapier, for example, uses usage as a primary lever for pricing. Their lowest tier is free, but you only get five zaps and 100 tasks per month. As you work up the tiers, they start to introduce more variables and the number of zaps and tasks increases. To be clear, the quality stays the same.

It's only the volume of product you get that changes. Amazon Prime, in contrast, is priced solely based on contract length. Their price goes down by 17% if you sign an annual contract. As products get more complicated, you begin to see variables grouped into meaningful buckets. The ideal pricing structure has at least one of each of these dimensions, with a limit set to target a specific use case. If we take another look at Zapier's pricing page, they've done a great job of labeling their pricing plans to appeal to different segments of their audience.

If I'm a company looking for an API connection tool, I know exactly where to go. Likewise, if I'm a one person operation and I just want my email to connect to a Google sheet, I know just where to go as well. I'm looking at an excerpt from the website that was mentioned, and there's several different tiers next to each other and in a big red box that has been outlined, the tiers are labeled free starter, professional team and company. If executed correctly. Tiered pricing strategies like this should provide value to the user equal to the price they're paying. Push users to upgrade to a higher tier as they begin to extract more value from the product.

Allow you to sell the same underlying product at different price points based on the value that your customer is going to get. For example, with Zapier, a company automating 100,000 tasks a month is getting a lot more value than a freelancer automating 750 tasks a month. Reward longer contracts since an annual upfront contract is effectively a loan with better pricing while also reducing churn. Since customers have already paid for a year, they'll be stickier. On top of these variables, Of course, is the role pricing plays in negotiations.

Discounting multi deals, favorable payment terms and more are all levers that salespeople can pull to close a deal. However, the core underlying structure of multi dimensional pricing remains intact and is, in our opinion, the best way to deliver maximum value to a range of customers at a range of prices.

How Much Pricing Your Product Part 2

Your price needs to align with your goal. Let's say you want to generate $1 million MSR and you're currently at 200,000 with 2000 customers. Let's also say that your target customer group has a population of 4000. Even if every single customer in the market was a customer of yours, you'd only be at 400,000 MSR. That may mean you need to raise your prices. Align your price with the value you create, not the cost of the value you create. Your price should not be a function of cost. It should be a function of the value you create.

Let's say it takes you one day to build a software program that saves a company millions of dollars. Would you only charge that company for a day's worth of work? No, because the value you created was much more than the cost. So while it's important to fold cost into the pricing discussion to make sure you're making enough money, it shouldn't be a major factor on the final sale other than to set a basement value. There is an example given there's a chart with. Two categories and bullet points.

The first category says monthly value and the bullet points read Fuel savings $1,000. Lubricant savings $100 savings from not needing to hire a contractor as frequently $200 incremental profit generated $200. Total value $1,500. Value created by the next best alternative $1,000. Incremental value. $500. The next category is monthly price. The bullet points read Price of next best alternative $750. 50% of the incremental value, assuming the value is split between you and the customer, $250. Price to customer $1,000. In the above example, our product creates $1,500 total value a month. The next best alternative creates $1,000 a month. So we're adding $500 of incremental value to get our price.

All we need to do is take whatever the competitor is charging $750 and add half the incremental value. We're now charging $1,000, which is more than the competitor, but the customer is still walking away with more value. $500 versus $250. Pricing tactics. For actionable advice based on solid academic research. I recommend googling Nick Kolenda for his list of pricing tactics. The nuances of your product may not align perfectly with this research, but it can serve as a starting point potentially for a B testing your pricing pages. Here are our favorite pricing tactics that we've used effectively. One. Kiss. Under that is a picture of a man sitting in a chair. And next to it is some text that says, "To build a great company, there are so many areas where you probably need to put effort into wanting to be very creative. But when it comes to pricing, don't be creative. Make it very, very simple.

Make sure your kids can understand that if you make the pricing too complex, I think you have a huge problem. That is a quote from Eric Wan, CEO and co-founder at Zoom. Your pricing should be dead easy to understand. Pricing is an extremely vulnerable point for the customer. They have to decide if the value you're promising is worth the price. The only way to make that decision is to understand exactly what you charge. Keep it simple, stupid. To anchor your price to something more expensive. Pretend that you've created a software product that replaces an employee whose job is to print labels onto boxes. There are two vastly different pricing approaches you could use here. One charge a price similar to other SaaS products that your target purchases $120 a month, or to charge half the price of that employee's wage $1,500 a month.

The second approach not only aligns your price with value, you also do it in such a way that you can easily justify your price to prospective customers. You just save them $1,500 a month. Three. Don't underestimate the power of pricing. One of the most fundamental concepts in economics is that demand increases as you lower your prices. I've witnessed firsthand just how massive an effect pricing changes can have on your sales performance. Your pricing web page might be one of the most frequently visited pages on your site, so testing and optimizing your pricing and packaging is well worth the effort.

For price discrimination. In general, people should pay for what they use. Or more precisely, for the value they receive. That's why it's important to charge people differently based on their needs. Traditionally, tech companies charge by the number of users. While this makes sense, in some contexts, it's often misaligned with the value created. For example, a small business might need three people accessing your software, but that doesn't mean they're willing to pay three times as much. But that business might be willing to pay three times as much if they started generating three times as much in revenue.

If your software enables the business to triple its revenue, then it actually makes sense for your price to increase alongside this revenue jump or some other metric like orders delivered. Packaging your services into bundles is another way to price discriminate. The key here is to make sure customers actually fall into each of the bundles. For example, you might have three packages: small business growth and enterprise. But it's possible that enterprise level customers are actually buying your small plan. That means that you've segmented your pricing incorrectly because you've assumed larger companies would want the bigger plan.

It could very well be that the larger companies value your large plan less because they already have a solution for 75% of the features offered. Five look for quick wins. Pricing is and should be a long and thoughtful process involving lots of different stakeholders. However, that doesn't mean that there aren't quick wins that you can exploit. For example, in one company I worked at, I changed the price of every product by a few cents so that everything ended in $0.99. This created over $100,000 in incremental revenue. Another time I tweaked the price online and created a record breaking marketing performance.

The key in both cases is that the pricing framework was principally agreed to with multiple stakeholders leaving me free to tailor the exact packaging and pricing in an agile way. With rapid AB testing. Ultimately, this led to a far better result than simply setting and forgetting. Chapter Summary Questions. What pricing model are you following? What levers are you pulling to change the price customers pay? Are you charging based on value, not on cost of service. Is your pricing entirely comprehensible in seven seconds or less? Have you linked your pricing to a higher value product? Have you constructed a system to test different pricing and packaging quickly and effectively to iterate on the best solution?

Have you agreed on the framework for your pricing and packaging? Do you have the buy-in trust and authority to run quick AB tests to find and capture additional revenue? 36. chapter Summary Exercise - Price What pricing model are you following? What levers are you pulling to change the price customers pay? Are you charging based on value, not on cost of service? Is your pricing entirely comprehensible in 7 seconds or less? Have you linked your pricing to a higher-value product?

Have you constructed a system to test different pricing and packaging quickly and effectively to iterate on the best solution? Have you agreed on the framework for your pricing and packaging? Do you have the buy-in, trust, and authority to run quick A/B tests to find and capture additional revenue?

Price Takeaway

Here are the main takeaways from this chapter. Your prices should align more with the value, create them with the costs you incur. Your prices should be dictated by the financial goals of your company, and you should avoid overly complicated pricing and packaging.

Common Problems Part 1

Bonus chapter Common Problems and their solutions. In this final chapter, we're going to cover the most common go to market problems that we see, along with actionable, practical advice on how to overcome them. You are not winning over new prospects in B2B product marketing If qualified leads or opportunities are not being won by the sales team, you should try to dig deeper into why that's happening.

To do this, you want to generate a report in Salesforce or a similar system. Look at the opportunities that are closed, lost and look at the reason codes. The reasons could be something like lost to competitor timing. Price is too high, not the decision maker missing features. Let's say that in the last six months the results were something like below. I'm looking at a table right now with two columns. The column on the left says Reason. The column on the right says Number of lost opportunities.

Lost a competitor 13. Timing is three, Price is too high is ten, not decision maker is two. Missing features are three. As you can see, the number one reason you are losing opportunities is because of your competition. You'll want to look deeper into this. Look at each opportunity in salesforce to identify which competitors show up the most. I'm looking at another table. With two columns.

The column on the left says competitor. The column on the right says the number of lost opportunities. A corp is nine, B

Corp is one, C Corp is three. As this table shows, a Corp is one of the leading reasons that you are not getting new sales. What you might find is that they offer a much lower price than you do. A sudden drop in website performance. One month I experienced a precipitous drop in performance of leads coming in from a website. That month I had changed the home page, but not without first running an AB test. Step one: Rerun the AB test.

The first thing I did was rerun the AB test yet again. My new homepage design performed better with a significantly higher conversion rate. Step two isolates the problem on the website. Looking more closely at where the conversion drop was most substantial, I noticed that the pricing page was the biggest contributor. This in and of itself was not proof that the pricing page was the problem. That's because people tend to convert on websites based on the entire website experience, not just the experience of one particular page.

So while the pricing page tends to generate a lot of conversions, all the other pages that the visitor sees contribute to the pricing page conversions. Step three, Isolate the problem at a broader level. Looking at the data for the past few months, I identified that pricing was the primary reason we were not closing prospects, particularly with respect to larger prospects. Step four: Talk to the internal team. I spoke to a business development rep, BDR, who told me that he was having a hard time selling our holistic software because the prospects already had software that did much of what we offered.

Step five: Look at external data. I looked at external data and found that about three fourths of larger prospects our new target already had software to do much of what we offered. Conclusion. The problem was that we had changed our pricing page in hopes of aligning better with our target customer, which was much larger than our previous target. Ironically, larger customers were actually quite price sensitive because they didn't value the holistic nature of our software as much. Since at that size they already purchased software to fix many problems.

We simplified our pricing structure and updated the pricing page to improve performance. Leads are up, but pipeline is down or leads are down, but Pipeline is up. A common psychological mistake humans make is associating recency with causation. This leads to problems with demand generation because metrics move on different timescales.

For example, your leads may be up for the month, but your pipeline may actually be down. That's because the pipeline for this month could be generated from last month's leads. Similarly, leads could be down this month, but pipeline may be up because lead generation last month was strong. It's important to measure results on the appropriate time scale.

If you've made a bunch of changes to your landing pages this month, then the appropriate gauge of success is improvements to your leads. Form submissions like these might be defined by marketing engaged leads in your company. The impact on the pipeline may not happen until the following month. Lots of leads, but sales aren't going up. This is a very common problem.

Marketers can have a very low standard for what constitutes a lead, whereas salespeople have a very high standard for what constitutes a lead. So what happens is all those top of funnel leads leak out in the middle.

For example, someone who watched a thought leadership webinar is not the kind of lead an account executive wants to talk to. The top and bottom of the sales funnel are easy. The real challenge is the middle of the funnel. For example, Mofu. Mofu. This is where you take the top of funnel leads, nurture them with educational content and warm them up so that they're willing to have a conversation with a sales person. See a demo or engage in some other high bar offer. A common way to do this is to provide a series of emails that educates the prospect on a specific pain point.

This might include a video case study of someone similar who overcame the problem. It could also include an email on best practices for overcoming that pain point. Eventually you have to sell the hard offer, which is the demo or consultation. In some cases there is an SDR sales development representative, also known as a BDR business development representative who sits in the middle between marketing and sales. The SDR might push the prospect to schedule a demo, or the marketer might. Increasingly, though, SDRs are reporting into marketing becoming another channel for marketers to play in.

Another problem might be even further down the funnel. When you're going to market, there are guaranteed to be some sales growing pains. As a go to market leader, your job is to make sure that sales have the capability to close the deals that marketing is delivering, which enters the world of sales enablement. Sales enablement is the process of building, delivering and maintaining the content processes, systems and tools that sales teams need to close business. Generally, sales enablement as a dedicated role will only happen after 50 to 75 sales reps are hired.

If you're going to market for the first time, then sales enablement will likely be owned by marketing, product marketing in particular. There are dozens of things you can do to try and improve your conversion rates. But for a first effort, content is your best bet. Specifically, you should produce internal content to help sellers have better, more relevant conversations. This kind of content might include won battle cards. Battle cards are a short document to help the account executives. Sales reps. Land sales.

The purpose is to prepare the sales reps to respond when customers ask about competitors. This can be a daunting task because the number of competitors could be endless and there could be very nuanced differences in features among the competitors. The mistake most marketers make is that they attempt to define their competitors based on whether they offer similar products. The first problem with this is that the competitive set can become too large. The second problem is that prospects will start naming competitors you've never heard of or ones you never thought were worthy to be considered competitors.

The main takeaway is that customers don't define competitors the same way your internal product team does. Instead, you should focus on who your bullseye target customer is and then let this definition narrow down the competitive set. You should also look at what competitors you're running into and losing deals to based on your CRM data. Once you've identified who the key competitors are, analyze them based on your value propositions. For example, if the main benefit of your product is that it speeds up assembly lines, then analyze your competitors based on that benefit.

Perhaps they are lacking certain key features that make their assembly lines move faster. Typically, marketers create a master table that details each of the competitors and the key features they have or don't have. I don't like this process because it's not customer centric. In sales conversions, customers will likely name just 1 or 2 key competitors rather than an exhaustive list. So I prefer to just go through each competitor one by one and identify their deficiencies in terms of delivering value. That way, the sales rep can quickly look at the specific competitor and speak about each issue.

Try to condense the information into a single sheet. In addition to providing the deficiencies for each competitor, make sure that your battle card speaks more broadly about where your product stands in the market. For example, you might say something like. Unlike most competitors, we offer 24 hour support. Or in general, our products save more in energy costs than most of our competitors. To the sales wiki. A sales wiki is just an aggregated, ideally searchable record for your sales team. All about the market, the product, the target customer and content to send and more.

This repository could include PowerPoint slides designed to educate the sales team on the target customer or other internal facing materials. It could also include customer facing materials such as handouts on specific product features or brochures catering to specific customer groups or buying personas. For example, you might have one handout for CEOs that talks about profit and loss and another handout for CTOs that talks about infrastructure integration capabilities.

Three. Crib notes. So part of the deliverable for sales enablement to help increase close rates and sales velocity is to condense it down into 1 to 2 sentences per point. If you can deliver it contextually when reps need it, that's even better. But the goal should be bite sized content pieces that are hyper relevant to the rep at a specific time. Crib notes are an easy way to deliver that value.

Large Customer

Large customers aren't buying. Often products go to market serving small companies. Then they ladder up to the mid market and finally to enterprise. This is a proven pathway for many SaaS companies. Because the needs of small companies or freelancers are usually less complex and the sales cycle is shorter. But their lifetime value is usually small.

So you would need to acquire a massive number of customers to build scale. It can be a lot easier to scale by serving enterprise clients. Once your product is sophisticated enough to meet their needs. It's worth noting, though, that these are not mutually exclusive. It's quite possible to serve both enterprise customers and small customers simultaneously. When I worked for a Google backed startup, we catered to micro companies, small medium companies, and also to enterprise clients.

You may find it difficult to sell to large companies for a number of reasons. They don't value your holistic solution. While small companies may have appreciated the breadth of your product, you may find that large companies already have specialized products to serve most of their needs. They've already developed systems and workarounds to get to the size they're at today. They've also already purchased products similar to yours. Your value proposition may actually narrow the further you move up the market.

You may need to focus more on one benefit that you deliver strongly on. They don't rationalize that customization is an option. Large companies may dismiss your solution because they don'trillionealize you offer thorough customizations to accommodate their workflows. You're too expensive. Ironically, large companies may actually be more price sensitive.

This isn't because they don't have money. It's because they simply don't derive as much value from your product as smaller companies do. You may have overestimated how much more large companies are willing to pay. You haven't enabled your account executives. Often larger companies have buying groups, and these may include multiple stakeholders who need to be sold to. As a marketer, you should develop selling tips that cater to each of those groups. For example, you may have an outline of the profit loss impacts of your products for CEOs or general managers and a technical product benefit sheet for engineering leads.

Event marketing is not producing qualified leads. Events can eat up the majority of the marketing budget for B2B companies. Investing tens of thousands of dollars on a single event is a risky investment. But the possibility of having keen buyers all grouped in a single place is too tantalizing for many companies to pass up. However, these big ticket events don't often lead to the same return on investment as low cost activities like webinars. So what's going on here? Your events are not targeted enough. Big events attract broad audiences who often don't care much for your product. You want to focus on events where the majority of attendees are your bullseye target customers, not just people who could buy our product, but the specific group that is most likely to buy it. Your event attendees aren't attending with intent.

Some events attract people to evaluate solutions and byproducts, but not that many. For most events, the draw to attendees is the education and sessions, not the opportunity to shop around the vendors. You want to either focus on events with the intent to buy or change the objectives of events. The majority of attendees are not customers. Sometimes the majority of attendees at events are not actually end buyers of your product. They may actually be potential partners or collaborators.

For example, the attendees may be web developers or professional service providers who cater to your end customers. You went to the event expecting new customers instead of building on your partner marketing. The attendees are not your buyers. For B2B tech companies in particular, the end user is often not the buyer. If the majority of your attendees are end users and not buyers, it's going to be difficult to have meaningful conversations.

For example, if you sell sales automation software, your end user might be an account executive, but your buyer is the VP sales VP marketing or VP operations. A conference where the attendees are sales reps isn't going to generate qualified opportunities. You've set the wrong expectations. Events have lots of auxiliary benefits beyond lead generation. Specifically brand awareness.

Essentially top of funnel impressions and deal acceleration events are really good at both these things. So as a savvy marketer, you may need to change the objective of your events to match what they're good at. PPC ads aren't producing the same results at scale. When you're small, you may see great results with PPC ads once you've properly optimized your keywords ads and landing pages. But at a certain point you may find that you cannot grow the advertising to get more customers cost effectively. What's happening here?

The thing with marketing tactics like Google ads is that they often work best at the bottom of the funnel. In other words, they cater to people who are already on the verge of buying a product like yours. But the size of the bottom of the funnel is always smaller than the top of the funnel. So it's very easy to saturate the bottom of the funnel with keywords like buy X or integration for Y. In my experience, PPC advertising is a baseline marketing tactic.

You run it continuously to capture the buy ready prospects, but the real growth will come from other tactics. For example, you may need to buy a list of 20,000 prospects and start hitting them with Facebook ads promoting your whitepaper. You then migrate those prospects into an email sequence and outreach that nurtures the leads to the point where they are pushed to the bottom of the funnel. PPC ads often just hit the low hanging fruit. Going to market without product or market fit. This problem is most common if you work for an early stage startup.

What happens is that you try to go to market before you truly have product market fit. That is, you haven't positioned yourself in a market where you have a proven track record of customers who love your product. That's large enough to achieve your revenue goals and where you can articulate your unique value over competitive alternatives.

Usually this step is rushed because a few early deals have closed and that drives assumed product market fit when in reality those deals are closed because of existing connections and founder selling rather than true evidence of a market in search of your solution. Companies rush into tactical execution and demand gen without having a strong foundation and end up spending ineffectively while they figure it out on the fly. Here are a few signs you might not have clear product market fit.

Every deal requires the founder, CEO, executive to be in on regardless of deal size. Long deal cycles for SMB mid-market deals. High customer churn rate. Extremely diverse customer user base. It's difficult to identify unifying factors. Low net promoter Score NPS. Or ideal client profile. ICP is only loosely defined. The only fix here is to go back, reassess your market options and find another niche that you can crack into with better success. Nobody is responding to my ads or emails.

Usually the problem here is that you're trying to promote your product company or brand instead of the offer itself. What I mean by the offer is your consultation, white paper, e-book, webinar, demo and so on. When you run direct response ads or emails, you need to sell the offer, usually with bullet points detailing the benefits of the offer. Nobody is responding to my Facebook or LinkedIn ads. When you're marketing on Facebook and LinkedIn, you're mostly marketing to cold leads who haven't heard of your company.

And that means you need to market a little differently. If your ads aren't converting, it's probably because you're trying to sell your company instead of your offer. If they've never heard of you, then you need to make sure they're getting value right away. Since there's no incentive for them to click on an ad about a company they've never heard of. Content that has a low commitment for them, like ebooks and white papers. Does this really well? Your ask is too high. Asking someone to attend an hour long webinar is a much higher ask than getting them to download an eBook. Try lowering what you want them to do.

You're asking for too much information. Response rates should improve if all you ask for is an email as opposed to name, email, company revenue, etcetera. There's too much friction in the user experience. Response rates should also improve if you use the lead gen forms built into the social platform instead of sending people to your own landing page. Especially for mobile traffic. We're losing too many deals to the competition. First, let's define how many is too many.

A good rule of thumb is that you should win between 35% and 45% of the opportunities you create. And of the 55 to 65% of deals that you lose, only about a third should be lost to competitors. That means if you create 100 opportunities, you'll win 35 of them, you'll lose 65 of them. And of that, you'll lose about 20% to a competitor. The rest you'll lose to other reasons. No decision, for example. So your aggregate competitor loss rate should be no more than 20% of all the opportunities you create. At most, if you're near or above this number, then you need to dig into the data and execute the relevant strategy.

I'm looking at another table on the left hand side. It says Questions to ask. And on the right hand side it says Strategic response. And it goes as follows. Are you losing deals from a specific segment, company size or industry response is to identify other segments where you're over indexing for one deal and shift your focus to there. If you can't, you need to dig into the specific needs of the market and reposition your product and marketing to serve it more effectively. Question: Are you losing the deals for a specific reason? Response. Invest in product development or pivot your product to an audience who doesn't have that specific requirement.

Question: Are you being priced out of the market? Response. Address your messaging to better convey the value you bring that is unique over the value your competitor can bring. Question: Are your competitors' sales processes much easier? Response. Streamline and simplify how you sell to make it easier for the buyer. Question. Is your customer experience worse?

Response. Talk to your happy and unhappy customers. What makes one happy or unhappy? Take those happy customers and replicate that success and tell that story during the sales cycle. That's the conclusion of the chart.

Conclusion

Conclusion. Taking a product to market isn't easy. Richard T James, the celebrated inventor of the Slinky, ended up living out his days in Bolivia while his extraordinarily talented wife ran the company as CEO. And yet products are launched every day. Teams are assembled, plans are made, audiences identified, and ads are bought.

At the very heart of this process is a fundamental belief that whatever new product you're launching or new feature you're selling is going to make life easier for your target audience. Going to market is just a process of convincing people that your new way is better than the status quo. Whether it's because they get to spend less time at work thanks to your solution, that makes them ten times more efficient or it's just a better light bulb. It doesn't matter.

As you go to market, your mission is to make your audience believe in what you're saying and to convince them to change from doing nothing to doing something. And to do that, you need to go through the seven steps to get to market. One. Identify your target audience. Two Outline the value you bring them. Three Figure out how to tell that story. Four Build your go to market team.

Five Define the demand and brand marketing channels that best reach your target audience. Six Calculate your marketing mix. And seven settle on a product price. Once you've gone through these steps and can cross off each one, then congratulations. You're ready to go to the market. You're ready to catapult your product into the waiting hands of your future customers.

You'll move your audience to action from doing nothing to doing something. You'll move your audience from not knowing, to not caring, to not buying, to finally, not even being able to comprehend living without your product. Once you make their life better, you'll know that you've gotten your product to market.

How to Market Yourself as a Coach or Consultant

Are you an independent Coach or Consultant who is just starting out in business?

Or perhaps you've been in business for awhile but you're not attracting enough clients or making enough money?

There's a lot that goes into building a successful Coaching or Consulting business.

In this book, I'll teach you exactly what you need to KNOW and DO to successfully market yourself as an independent coach or consultant.

I look forward to seeing you in the book and helping you market your coaching or consulting business!

Introduction

Our objective is to create, innovate and deliver a difference for your business from getting your product online, selling to the right customers and developing custom applications for your business processes.

I believe we must all aspire to live a life that brings fulfillment in our work and one that helps others realize meaning in their lives and work when we do this. It's a win-win situation and we get what we want while helping others get what they want. This Book has been designed with you in mind, and you'll be happy to know that I have personally walked every step of this Book in my career, which has led to what I do now.

I would not be teaching or showing you anything that I have not personally experienced and executed for myself. In this Book, you will learn why it's important to think beyond employment or being an employee and start seeing yourself as an owner, an expert or whatever you want to become. You will learn why it's not just about the money that you make as a consultant, but also about the freedom you get and the experience you create for your clients.

We will talk about the things that you must check off before you venture into consulting. And finally, when we get to the meat of the discussion, I will show you how to put all of these things in place to ensure that your success as you transitioned from an employee to consultant is guaranteed as a bonus. I'll also be bringing one of my respected friends who has had a remarkable journey and success as a consultant to share stories, ideas and best pieces of advice with you. So why don't we get started?

Why You Should Learn From Me and This Book

Before we get started, I think it's important that we establish trust and that you feel confident about this journey that you're about to embark on. My first Johnny and experience as a consultant started nearly 10 years ago when I started an entertainment

consulting brand. I've seen firsthand the pitfalls and the secrets to launching a career as a consultant. And in the years that I've been operating as a consultant or as a director have experienced the highs and the lows of the process, which I'm going to share with you to give you a head start and help you avoid the common errors that most people make when transitioning from an employee to a consultant.

Today, I am the director of three major consulting outfits, one in e-commerce business, another one in personal development, and one in 2010. So I have put all of my experiences into this Book for you with a point of view that spans three uniquely different industries where you can successfully operate as a consultant. And that combined with an industry specific experience that my guest will offer you in this Book, ranging from tech to health to beauty and creative industries.

If you're tired of your job, if you hate going to work, if you would rather do something else for your bills were paid, if you feel as though you could be doing something more exciting and more fulfilling and more meaningful with your life, then I believe you have chosen the right Book to help you eliminate these problems because you deserve to live an exciting, fulfilling and meaningful life. And no lifestyle or bills should get in the way of that.

The fact that you're here means that you are ready to resolve this problem and avoid future consequences that may be harder, if not impossible, to correct down the line. We don't want a future that is financially secure and there's nothing wrong with that. But to realize that the work must start now wherever you are in your journey. The time to start is now. Transitioning from an employee to a consultant will not solve all of your life's problems. Let's settle that right now. But it will surely put you in a position where you have more control over your time, your energy and your resources, both financially and otherwise.

And this is the kind of life you want, the life that you leave on your terms, pursuing the things that are personally important to you and spending your time and energy with people and places you choose. I like to say this way. Everyday choices have been made in our lives, but the difference is who is chosen for us? Would you like to be the one choosing how much money you can make? Would you like to be the one choosing how much time you spend working? Would you like to choose people you work with and spend time with? And the time to make those choices for yourself starts right now.

Things You Need to Know to Go From Employee to Consultant (ROR

I'm sure there are many industry definitions for what consulting is or what it isn't. But I want to simplify it and make it as simple as possible for you as this will be very important, super important to understand from the perspective of value rather than function. Being a consultant is more about the value you add, not the job of the task that you perform. So this is my definition.

Consulting is when your work is defined by the value it has to your customers as opposed to the actual work function that you perform. Anyone can perform a task and get a job done. Imagine as an employee, if you're an employee right now, your company pays you to perform the tasks and get work done and you never have to. If you're not willing to step into the role of adding extra value to the customers that you serve beyond your job requirements.

But as a consultant, your primary job is to add value even before you put your hands to do any work whatsoever. So adding value from the point of contact with your potential customers is what will differentiate you from other consultants out there? I like the way John C. Maxwell puts it. He said leaders touch your heart before they ask for a hand.

In other words, your first objective as a consultant is connecting with your clients at the heart level before asking for the work. And that happens when you approach them with something of value that they can use right now, today. No obligation. So let's look at the specific things that you will need to know first before we get down to the nitty gritty of building your consulting work. Number one, the problem you're most passionate about solving.

The second thing you need to know, the marketable skills that you possess to solve this problem. The thing you need to know is the marketable skills that you can learn to solve the problem. And the fourth thing is the relationships you need to leverage to build your brand and finally the resources you need to leverage to equip your brand for success. If you notice something, none of these prerequisites include money, capital or income. And that's on purpose because money is not your focus and it should never be your priority.

Money will come as a byproduct of the value you add in the experiences you create for your clients. Later in this Book I will look into each one in detail to help you understand why it's important to know these things from the start and how to implement each one of them. Now, let's talk about the practical ways to go from being an employee to a consultant. This is where the rubber meets the road. This is where we work on the prerequisites we've developed or we're developing so far by digging deeper into each one and executing the task required to bring them to life.

Also, we will look into other ideas and strategies to help you succeed as you go along. As a consultant, the next most important thing you will need after deciding the problem you want to solve is that a management consultant demands a high level of management of what I refer to as R, which stands for your resources, your opportunities and your relationships. These are the things you would often have in short supply, especially at the start of your journey as a consultant.

So you have to learn how to manage them extremely well to grow and succeed as a consultant. So let's take a look into these management concepts ahead of your implementation plan. The first thing we're going to look at in the arrow, our management and what differentiates a successful consultant and those that are struggling is how you manage things. To become successful as a consultant, you will need to pay extreme attention, particularly to the following things. Number one, your resources.

You are no longer being paid by someone else. So you have to be intentional with how you spend your time, what you spend money on and any tools to acquire for your work. This is why your resources are so, so important. And even if you still have your job on the side, you want to act and think like the job doesn't exist. You want to not focus or rely on the security from that job. You want to approach your resources and save the business is all you've got for financial security. Sometimes it is smarter to rent instead of buying.

And you also find that in the beginning you may not need all the fancy tools of software that are commonly seen in an established business. I remember a story where I started a studio to teach students and I put so much money into this venture that it didn't succeed. You know why? Why? Because

I was heavily financially invested too soon. You need to start with what you have instead of going off to rent an office space, walk from home when you start.

If your line of work requires a space outside of your home, try coworking or shared spaces as much as possible. It is best to put your time and money towards efforts that will generate work and nuclides, and once you have steady income and work and repeat customers, you might be able to spend a little more on things you may need to enhance your work. The bottom line is this to focus on activities that reduce expenses but increase income.

ROR Management (Cont'd)

The next thing you have to learn how to manage really well is your opportunities. So the management of opportunities are critical to succeeding. As a consultant, you need to learn to look at every project as a seed that can produce more work for you. And when you approach your work this way, you will have plenty of opportunities that keep giving. When I started my I consulted in the first five projects that I worked on were from two clients. This is why it's important to leverage every client you get and be proactive at seeing opportunities where they can help the client.

There are always problems to be solved even when they don't see it. There's always something that can be optimized, done more efficiently. And that's where you come in training yourself to see opportunities on behalf of your clients. And they would love you for it. I know it's common knowledge that it's easier to get repeat business from existing clients than it is to get new business from new clients. So when you learn to manage your opportunities well, you can count on repeat business. And I can tell you this from experience. I've I've I've enjoyed up to six years of repeat business from some of my clients in the entertainment space by not sharing the opportunities and seeing more areas for improvement.

Now, the final area where you need to learn to manage is relationships. Managing relationships well as a consultant is similar to how you manage opportunities. But the difference here is that the relationships in nature are going to serve as the lifeblood of your business. And when it comes to relationships, especially if you are consulting in the same field you worked as an employee, the most important ones to nurture are those of your previous employers and colleagues. If you do this well, your employer becomes your client and your colleagues generate free water mouth marketing for you.

In my experience, I partnered with my previous employer and continued to serve their clients as a consultant, which means we both win. They still get to leverage my years of experience for their business and I get to serve their clients. I get to keep work coming in for me. So you need to learn to see your relationship with your employer from that perspective. Most companies have programs or partnership arrangements where you can go into and still support them as a consultant.

Also, on several occasions, many of my colleagues who knew about my new venture, they put in a word for me here and there, and I have retained high value clients from these referrals. So here's the bottom line. Your employer is not your competition. When you decide to become a consultant, you need to make them your sales channel. And as a new consultant, this is priceless.

The Problem

The first thing we need to look at is the problem that you're most passionate about solving, and I think it was Albert Einstein who said we cannot solve our problems with the same level of thinking that created them. And that is why most people can't solve their problems, because the solution requires them to think differently. And at a higher level, which is where you come in, there is something you're good at doing and that solves a problem for others.

You might already be working in that capacity on your job or as an employee, but it's time to take that solution out and stand on your own so that you can help more people. And this doesn't mean you have to quit your job right away as you can run your consulting side by side, which is a full time job until you're ready to make the full transition, because this is very important for key financial reasons. So the first thing you need to do is write down the problems you want to solve.

Others have provided a worksheet with this Book that you can use to write this down. So that you can keep all your ideas in one place when you have done this thing where you have this list of problems you want to solve, return to this Book to continue. Now we're going to do a little market research on your problem. The best way to approach solving any problem is to understand the two key players that work in every industry, the best providers and the best solution. This will save you from trying to reinvent the wheel and help in using already available resources to your advantage.

Google is your friend, so reach out and do a keyword search for the top service and product provider in the industry where you're going to be solving problems. Secondly, do a quick search for the best tools, the best products and solutions currently available

for this problem. In my case, I wanted to help online business owners streamline the sales channels with the accounting system. So my research was something like, you know, looking at the best e-commerce platforms or most widely used e-commerce platform.

This gives me the information to the top service providers that most of my existing and potential clients are already operating on. And I can use this information to strategize my campaigns when it comes to marketing my services to the new clients. The second thing is I looked at the best tools for online business accounting, this key research helped me see the top accounting packages that online retailers are using, and that gives me the opportunity to come in as the middleman who connects the accounting packages to the e-commerce platforms.

Again, this is just an example of what I do, and I understand it will be different from what you are going to do. So make sure to tailor your research to your products and services and the tools that are already available to solve your problems. Your business might be an exception where you are creating the products or tools to solve the problems, even in this case. Make sure you understand the current reality of the industry you operate in so you can position yourself in your solution to receive the best adoption possible when you come on the scene, I hope, and now you're feeling a little bit more confident about your problems and the solutions you're going to provide. Next, we're going to look at the practical skills that you need to make this work.

Marketable Skills

Now that we've determined the problem, do you want to serve as a consultant? The next thing we are going to do is look at the marketable skills that you already possess to solve this problem. And just in case you're still a little fuzzy about the problem you want to solve, there's no need to worry. We can look at that from a different angle. And that's what we're about to do here.

What is something you do well that people will pay for? This also points back to the problem you are already equipped to solve for others. I'll put it another way. What are the things that you see all the people do and get paid for that you can also do well or even better? In other words, if all this is getting paid for doing it, so can you. So what I need you to do is write down the top five marketable skills that you possess. That you can use to solve the problems that you've identified in this process, where you have this list, return to this Book and continue. It is important to solve problems that you have the aptitude and passion for, not just problems that are common, lucrative or easy to find.

When clients pay you for service or product, they expect you to deliver your best because they chose you out of many options out there. And this is why it's even more important to get this solution down pat. It cannot be half baked. So what are you what are you most good at doing, what problems, how your top five skills related to this is your treasure and once you determine what they are, then applied to market research steps that we talked about earlier to make sure you're approaching the right customers and providing the relevant solutions for most people, you may not already possess some of the skills that you need to solve the problems that you want to solve as a consultant.

So this is where this session comes in, the marketable skills that you can learn to solve your problems. If you're not well skilled to solve the problem you are most passionate about, then you need to determine the skills that you need to be competent enough to solve the problem. When I started, I had the passion to work with and help businesses streamline and simplify the processes. But I had to study to be competent at solving business information system problems. So for me, this came in the form of getting certified to provide application, deployment, management, training and support services on the Salesforce platform.

And of course, this was in addition to all the knowledge and skills that I have already acquired from my years of working in the service field of my specialty. So what I'm saying is you need to sit down and write down the skills that you would need to learn to become competent at solving the problems you identified in steps one or two. And when you've done this, we need to explore the learning channels available for these skills. When you have completed this list, return to this Book and continue.

Marketable Skills II

When it comes to skills, it'll come down to two unique categories, soft and hard skills. You know, your soft skills are, you know, like whatever we've already covered, like management and people skills. On the other hand, you need skills that are actually measurable and teachable abilities that you will need to possess to carry out your work from day to day, like your programming skills or your plumbing skills, your medical skills, whatever that is for you.

Defining the skills you need will decide where you go to acquire it. As a consultant, unlike an employee, your customers would care less about your bachelor's and master's degree and more about your ability to solve their problems. So as a result, you can acquire many of these hot skills you would need through self training or online resources for professional development. Let's say you're a photographer and you're going into full time consulting. Your clients are now going to care about whether you have a photography degree or they will want to see the quality of your work, though.

And you can count on that. And I can tell you personally that I know many photographers who have never been to the four walls of a college, but they've mastered their craft through self training and often through online resources. Depending on your business, you two can do the same. The goal is to be competent in Problem-Solving and providing the solutions people will pay you for so that upskilling in the areas you need to be competent at the earliest possible as your journey progresses in transitioning to a consultant. Next, we're going to look at how to leverage the relationships you already have to build your brand.

Brand Relationships

Now, let's talk about the relationships that you need to leverage to build your brand. This is really, really important. There's a saying I've heard over and over again in one of my MBA classes, and he goes something like, relationships are more important than product knowledge. People don't really care about how good you are or what you know about the product.

If you are unable to build relationships and speak of relationships, you have to learn to manage two different sides. One is your clients. On the other side are your partners or allies in business. So let's talk about your clients. Nobody cares how much you know until they know how much you care. So the question is, do you genuinely care about your client's success?

Do you look at the business and only see dollar signs or do you see opportunities to help them succeed? This is something that people can tell when they start to talk to you. I remember having a client who I've worked with for over three years now, and we've built a very good relationship so much that every time I get on the phone with us right now, we talk about life stuff in personal things before we even talk about business.

And that's where you want to get to, where you connect with people before you do business, where you put people before business, you get more business from people. So now let's look at the relationships to do with your allies or your business partners. It's not enough to know the problem you want to solve or be competent at solving it. You also need to find the right people to collaborate with and learn from in the process of establishing yourself as a respected consultant.

When I decided that I needed to become a Salesforce consultant as an administrator, I reached out to the in-house sales force specialist, my last full time job, and sought his advice. And he was very kind to the point that he pointed me in the right direction, which eventually led to me getting all the information and the resources that I needed to become certified. So ask for help as people are always willing to help when you ask.

Now, the next thing I need you to do is to write down the names of five people that you can learn from. I work as a consultant using the worksheet provided in this Book. And once you've done that, we'll go on to the next step.

Brand Relationships and Resources

The next step is to tap into these relationships, to help you develop knowledge and skills and have the brain power and establish trust with your potential clients. So here are some things that you can do right now to maximize these five relationships. Number one, you can set up a meeting. And secondly, you can visit them at the business and see the wrong things.

You can ask for referrals when they are over capacity with their clients. And lastly, which is the most important thing, you need to stay in touch and keep learning from these people when they see your drive and consistency, don't feel more confident about you and your work, which leads to more collaboration in the future. The next thing we're going to look into right now is the resources you're going to need to leverage to equip your brand now that you know what your problem is, the skills you possess or need to learn, and the people you need to succeed.

It's time we look at the operation of your consulting outfit. One of the things is, who are the people you would need to run the day to day operations of your work as a consultant? Some of these resources you already have on know and some you may need to acquire or leverage from others. When I started my entertainment consulting outfit, I needed entertainers, you know, singers, musicians, dancers.

The agency needed these people to run its operations for our clients. In the same way, with my I.T. consulting, I needed contacts, I needed referrals, I needed application access to ensure the efficiency of my operations. So right now, what I need you to do is use the worksheet provided with this Book and write down the resources, the things and the people that you will need for the operation of your consulting outfit. And depending on the field that you want to consult in, most of these resources may already be at your disposal. So please pay attention to that.

But first things first, ensure that you have the following, make sure that your business is registered. Depending on your location and regulations around business registrations, this information is just a Google search away. Or you can hire an accountant to say this. I love you for a fee. Accounting is hugely important to keep your business alive. And unless you're a professional accountant or with a solid background in accounting, I do not recommend doing your finances yourself.

But I do recommend saving an account in expenses by using one of the many available accounting and payment applications for small businesses like Quickflix. Zero square payments, to name a few. These are all Web based applications and to make it easier to get paid to invoice your clients and to keep track of your expenses and keep up to date accounting records, which you can easily turn over to a professional accountant at the end of financial periods for business tax purposes. But always take your accountant's advice for the best option possible.

Another important resource for your brand is an online presence. You need to be accessible online, and particularly where your customers go. Always remain visible and engaged where your ideal customers are found. This could be Facebook groups. It could be online forums, business network groups, or your local chamber of Commerce. The cost of online branding and advertising can rack up really quickly and crippling to a small business. Therefore, you have to be resourceful and leverage free to some, some of which you will need to learn how to use to get your business up and running at the early stages.

Learning how to use these free tools will give you the opportunity to generate things like brand materials, like logos and flyers or like images for your business, whatever it is that you may need. It's also important to take advantage of job building sites extensively, for example, like work or reputable online business forums where you can succeed and give advice. And the key is staying consistent on these platforms, because this will give you visibility and credibility with local businesses as well as potential clients. The second thing I want to talk about here, reinforcing the idea in some of the things that I've already mentioned, is the importance of setting aside a specific number of hours every week for professional development.

As a consultant, you don't have the luxury of, you know, having people do things for you. And this is why it's so important to learn to do a lot of things yourself. And the only way you learn to do this is by having a consistent habit of planned activities where you go to learn specific things relating to your business. I can recall when I was trying to become a salesforce certified administrator, I spent three months every day spending five to six hours just studying and learning about this platform. Took me three months.

What normally takes people like 12 months or 24 months. And that was because it was very important for me that I learned this aspect of the system for me to succeed as a consultant. So this is also very important for you. Make sure you have set aside time to do professional development each and every week. So the last thing I want to mention when it comes to relationships and resources is you have to learn to not pay for things you can do for yourself. It's important.

Do not pay for things you can learn to do for yourself, because as being a consultant, one of the themes and one of the most important things that set you apart is your ability to learn and obscure yourself and acquire as many skills as possible in your business so that you can limit the activities that generate expenses and increase the activities that generate income.

Pricing Your Products and Services

Now, let's talk about pricing your products and services. This is really, really important, and I'm sure you're probably wondering why it took so long to get to this part. It's something important that we need to talk about when it comes to deciding or determining how to price your products and services.

The first thing you want to do is do your market research and know the rates in the market that you operate in. And if you're a web developer, you need to know how much your competitors are charging for the same sort of size of jobs that you do, because if you don't know you, you run the risk of either overpricing your products or on the price and your services.

And this is super important to know. So the first thing is to do your market research and be familiar with the rates industry that you operate. And the next thing you want to do is to look at your competitors and look at what they're doing in terms of price and in value. Like I said before, at the beginning of this program, the most important thing as a consultant is the value that you're adding to your clients. So be sure that when you create your price, when you are looking at your price strategy, make sure that you're using value to determine what the price should be, because at the end of the day, people will pay more when they get better value.

So you need to understand it and make sure that your position and your price and from the point of view of value, but also knowing what your competitors are doing. So that way you give yourself an opportunity and a leverage to beat that. When it comes to actually charging fees in three different ways. You can approach this. You can use a retainer fee, you can use a fixed fee, or you could charge by the hour, depending on what the circumstance of the situation is.

If you have an ongoing contract and ongoing management consulting or service with a client, it makes a lot of sense to put them on a retainer fee. If you have a project where you can determine the start and the end date of the project, you can charge a fixed fee. And if you have, clients will come to you every two weeks or every month, every three months, you know, to request work, you can look into charging clients like that by the hour because then that makes a lot of sense to you and it gives you the opportunity to maximize your profit from jobs like that.

Finally, on pricing your products and services, the most important thing you want to remember is you need to be profitable. The purpose, the whole reason behind all of this is so you can have a profitable business. And this is why I said earlier that you need to focus on activities that generate income and decrease expenses and this is how you become profitable. So always remember when you said in your prices, be profitable.

Meet David Donohue

My name is David Donahue, the managing director of Donehue Consultancy. So when I first started this business, I didn't anticipate getting into consulting at all. All I knew was that basically I wanted to work for myself. It's been quite a bit of a journey leading up to where I've got to so far. I guess it really started when I got really interested in the startup startup community. I worked at a Nemer startup community around Brisbane just learning what it was to run a business and to see what other people were doing in this sort of space. Uh, it was quite a difficult learning curve because I saw a lot of failures in business. So I guess the tough side of running a startup, essentially running a startup, you don't have a lot of money. So we were living on rotten noodles.

We were pretty much living on peanut butter, and couldn't even afford the bread. So we went from that and pretty much living day to day. And eventually I got picked up by a small startup in Brisbane who actually just recently received venture capitalist funding. So I went to join that company and it really introduced me to e-commerce. So when I joined the company, I was part of the support team. I basically spoke to customers day to day, dealing with businesses day to day.

And that was the most I think for me that was the most interesting part, because I got to understand how business works and where things sort of fell short and I really started to enjoy making things better for customers. So something was taking someone three hours to do every day. I was able to turn it into a two minute job and I got real satisfaction out of that. Unfortunately for me, I was in a position where I couldn't spend a lot of time with customers.

I had numerous responsibilities and things like that. And eventually what I did was I asked my boss, he said, I want to go out on my own and actually be a consultant. At first he thought I was a bit crazy. He's like, You sure you want to leave a job to go on your own? It's not easy. And I said, yeah, I actually do. And it was a huge risk for me and my partner simply because we wouldn't know where our next paycheck was going to come from. But looking back on it now, we're three years in and it was the best decision I ever made.

What's The #1 Biggest Lesson You've Learned As A Consultant?

The biggest chapter for me is understanding your value. So and never compromise on the value that you provide, if you truly believe you're an expert in something, charge accordingly. And don't let people negotiate on your costs no matter what. It's the people who appreciate the service that you do that will actually end up paying for that sort of service.

So it's quite easy to get in a situation where you might feel desperate or you might need more work and things like that, and you might decide to, you know, work with someone who won't appreciate exactly what you do. And that only leads to more problems. So the biggest number one thing I guess I could sort of say is, obviously understand your own value and stick to your guns in that regard.

What's Your #1 Advice For Someone Transitioning Into Consulting?

I guess the biggest bit of advice I can give is to become an expert in something. This is not one of those things that's sort of like fake it till you make it. You really have to become a real expert in something. So you need to immerse yourself. You need to educate yourself.

The biggest thing is you need to work in an industry where you understand what's out there, what the problems are. Until you can do that, then you're not going to become a real expert and you can't really add value. So I always say working in the industry first so that you can get the experience that you need to go out and become that expert.

So that way, when you're speaking to customers, you know exactly what they're after, what their pain points are, and then you can tackle those problems straight away.

What's Your #1 Advice For Someone Transitioning Into Consulting?

As a consultant, the most important skill that you can have is to be a good communicator. So you need to constantly communicate with your clients and be clear and precise with what you're saying to them. So remember that you are not a consultant. You're an educator at the end of the day. And if you're educating your clients, they're going to be your students.

So you think back to a schoolroom situation where your teacher gives you instructions, a clear set of instructions and a clear format to do things. And that's the way you need to sort of treat your clients. You know, you need to make sure that you're always communicating with them, always being proactive with them so that they understand exactly what they're doing and they understand the value of the.

Industry-Specific Advice For The Tech Space As A Consultant

The biggest piece of advice I can give is don't be mediocre. I say that, and that's quite blunt to say, but there are a lot of people out there who fail to give good customer service. I feel like that's where the space really lacks and that's where you can really define yourself and differentiate yourself from the market. So you see it time and time again where good customer service begins at the sale. People are happy you're communicating well. And as soon as they hit that buy button, all communication gets lost.

It's like you've gone over that hump. You've gone, oh, yeah, we got the style. OK, great. I can now sit back and enjoy life. It's like, no, you need to be proactive with those customers. You need to show that you are listening to them and giving it by listening to the feedback they provide you as well. So you can give an optimal service to your customers at all times. And that's really how you get customers for life. And that's the most important thing, is making sure you've got good customers. Loyalty is the end of the day. If you start building up a loyalty base, they will sell the services for you.

Further Advice

The main piece of advice I'd give for any business consultant would be when you're building up your business to make sure you're consistent with your clients because people want to see the exact same process every single time. If you start showing inconsistencies in your business that gives uncertainty to two clients, I feel like all the services have changed. It's not as good as what it used to be. Or maybe one time I got really good service and another time I got a pretty subpar level of service.

And when you give customers uncertainty, they don't know what the future holds for them. So always develop a foolproof system for your business and always continue to refine your business processes to ensure that, you know, you've got that level of consistency for your customers and something that they would appreciate.

Book Recommendation

One recommendation I would give to people who are building a foolproof business model would be to read the email by Mark Zuckerberg. Mark Zuckerberg explains the importance of building a foolproof system within your business, which is really going to pay off for your customers.

Recap and Final Words

Thank you so much for enrolling in this Book. I just want to say thank you for being a part of it and I hope you've learned something. I hope you have gained some information and knowledge from this that you can now take with you to start your journey as a consultant. Just to recap some of the things that we talk about so that you don't forget.

Now, the most important thing is to know the problem that you want to solve and then know what skills you have to solve those problems and then understand what relationships and what resources are going to be key in determining how you need to run your business. So if you don't remember anything from this program, always remember that relationships are more important than product knowledge.

It's important that you maximize your leverage and you nurture your relationships with your clients as well as your partners or business allies, because these are the things that are going to sustain you and ensure that you continue to make profit as a consultant and in your business.

Digital Marketing Fundamentals Beginner to Pro

Digital Marketing Mastery will give you the skills, strategy, and resources that will allow you to confidently create marketing that drives results and the ability to grow ANY business.

You'll discover the proven principles that all great marketing campaigns are built on and learn how to create killer campaigns of your very own.

Learn how to tap into a never ending supply of content ideas and create high converting content that makes sales without sounding "salesy" and the secret to overcoming objections in advance.

Identify and target your perfect market online and create the most effective social media marketing campaigns using today's most popular platforms.

Design and build your own automatic customer-generating marketing funnel and discover the simple strategy that guarantees profitability right from the very first click.

Email marketing is one of the most effective and profitable tools available to today's modern digital marketer. This will show you exactly how to make email your email list your most valuable asset. Ever.

Data is what separates the amateurs from the pros. Discover the most important digital marketing metrics to track and create your very own digital marketing metrics tracking sheet.

Above all else...

Digital Marketing Mastery will give you the skills, strategy, and resources that will allow you to confidently create marketing that drives results and the ability to grow ANY business.

Introduction to Digital Marketing with LinkedIn

Welcome to part one, Bottom of Funnel. A LinkedIn Marketing. An overview of what we're going to be discussing in Part one is here on the agenda. We're going to start with an introduction to give a high level overview of how to approach the bottom of the funnel. Then we're going to get into message and conversation ads, which are the LinkedIn ads that go directly to people's inboxes and look kind of like you're getting a message.

Now we're going to talk about Sales Navigator and outreach. So doing things like cold email, LinkedIn message automation, connection requests, that sort of stuff. Then we're going to get into image and video ads, which are the more standard types of advertisements that people usually think of when they talk about LinkedIn marketing. Then we're going to get into text ads, which were the original type of ads that LinkedIn had way back when I started in 2011 that look kind of like Google ads, but have little images, and then we'll talk about some other concepts. So part one focuses on lead generation.

Now, whenever you create a new campaign and LinkedIn, there are basically three buckets of objectives that you need to take a look at. And this is one of the biggest considerations that you need to have when you start advertising on LinkedIn is what is the objective that you want? All too often people jump into strategies and tactics, but they don't really know where they want to go. So this is the high level decision you need to make. And what we're going to do in chapter one is we're going to focus primarily on lead generation as an objective as one of the subcategories of conversions.

Now there's one ad type, the tax ads, where we pretty much have to use the website conversions option at the bottom of the funnel. But for the most part, we're using lead generation and the lead generation objective is going to allow us to use the lead capture form and linked in itself rather than needing to send people to our website or landing page. Now at a high level when we look at budgeting, which is like the biggest decision you're going to make with your media, media spend, we need to think about what are the most successful businesses to business companies and those that are really fast growing.

They basically allocate their budget in two different ways. So one is sales activation or what you might call capturing demand. So this is the conventional demand generation, lead generation. Let's generate a lot of revenue really quickly. Let's get people into sales conversations, that type of marketing. On the other hand, there's what you might call brand marketing, creating demand, and that's an aspect of marketing that is also often neglected, particularly by large business to business companies. But you can see that the split is almost 5050 now.

The optimal is 54% of your budget being allocated to capturing demand. So things like demand generation and 46% being spent on creating demand. Now what I would actually say is if you're in a small startup, this percentage should actually be higher. You're probably looking at more like 75%, potentially even higher, allocate it to things that are going to generate revenue basically in the next six months or generate pipeline revenue, sales, qualified opportunities in the next six months. And then you might allocate, say, 25% towards long term growth, at least focused on long term growth.

And that's things like building your brand, building your community, working through dark social channels, stuff like that. So what we're going to do in part one, because this is where a slight majority of your budget and energy should be focused, is really on capturing demand, short term revenue growth. Now, it might seem a little bit counterintuitive. Why am I starting at the bottom of the funnel? And to explain that, we're going to use this framework from Salesforce.

Now, on the left here is a conventional marketing funnel. You start with the call leads, which is like your largest quantity of prospects. Then you move and start focusing on the warm prospects. And then at the bottom, you focus on the hot ones, the ones that are about to buy. But what Salesforce does is they flip this funnel on its head and they say, Well, maybe what we should really do is focus on the hot leads first, right?

The low hanging fruit, the people that could be buying very soon. And then we can start worrying about the people that maybe potentially will buy in the midterm and then after that will focus on the core leads of the people that may buy in the long term. Now, what Salesforce is really talking about is emails like where should you focus your emails? But I'm going to extrapolate this and say that at a high level, this is really what you should be doing. And the reason is because if you don't have a lot of resources and you don't have a lot of patience, let's say you're a small company with a low budget or a mid-sized company that needs to generate revenue this year or this quarter.

Really, you need to focus on those activities that are going to generate revenue quickly. And that is the bottom of the funnel. That is those hot leads. And that's what we're going to be talking about in this part of the Book. And then next, if you have time and you know that your company is going to be around for a couple of years, and you know that you can carve out a portion of your budget, allocate it towards capturing demand in the midterm. Then you can start worrying about the warm leads and then ultimately the cold leads, which you might reach through a long term thought leadership and stuff like that.

All too often there's a problem that companies make. So small companies, what they do is they start at the top of the funnel. They generate all sorts of cool brand marketing thought leadership, but it never actually converts to revenue. And the reason it doesn't is because you need to first build a system to capture demand at the bottom of the funnel. And you also need to allow enough time for this to convert to revenue. And for small companies, unfortunately, they just can't really focus much here.

Large companies have the reverse problem. So often they got large or they got to the mid-sized. By focusing on demand generation, on the hot leads, they generate IT revenue, and then they think, okay, well that worked in the past, so let's just keep doing that. Let's just keep doing what's measurable, what's been proven, really. They're better off getting a much larger portion of people into their funnel by focusing on those cold leads at the top of the funnel here. So let's focus on the hot leads in this chapter.

Now, the framework that I like to use for business to business marketing and this framework could also apply if we're just talking about building a LinkedIn advertising campaign or a LinkedIn marketing campaign if we want to think about creating ads and content for each stage of awareness. And I broke the stages of awareness into six chapters. So we have the top of the funnel, which has two chapters, the middle of the funnel, the Mo Mofo, which has two chapters, and the bottom of the funnel, the bow, which also has two chapters. So let's talk about the tofu topic.

First, we have people that are brand unaware. Now, when I talk about your brand, I'm not talking about your product. I'm not talking about your features. I'm not talking about those nitty gritty things. What I'm talking about is literally your brand. So your logo, your mascot, your slogan, the kinds of things that people remember, whether or not they understand how your product works or what it does. Do they know your brand and they know your logo? A good example. This would be something like a loom.

I was looking for screen capture software recently and I saw a loom. I didn't really know what they did, but I recognized the logo and I said, Oh, okay, I will. I'll try that out. I recognize the name. Okay, so that's brand honor where people that don't know your name, they don't know your logo, etc. Now we have another category of people at the top of the funnel that aren't really aware of the problem that you solve, or they're not convinced that whatever problem you solve is a priority. It's something they should really put at the top of their priority list and act on it now. So next, as we move into the middle funnel, we have people that are category on Aware.

So they're familiar with the problem they have, but they don't necessarily know that your product category and maybe that's chatbots, maybe that's certain manufacturing automation equipment, whatever that category is that you and your competitors are in. They don't they aren't necessarily convinced that's going to solve their problem or is the best solution to their problem. Now we're getting into what most people understand, which is being a product . Where do people understand your use cases, your jobs to be done, your features, your benefits?

Are they convinced you're better than the competition? Are they convinced that you can solve their problem? Better than the competitors can. Now, a lot of people understand this, but they understand that sometimes what people really need to be convinced of is that the problem is worthy of attention and that the category in general is worthy of attention. Now, at the bottom of the funnel, we have a free offer on Aware. So your free offer is going to be some examples that I have below here. It's your consultation, your trial, your review, your audit.

You might call it something else, but basically it's the thing that's designed to either get to a sales conversation or sort of get into that sales activity mindset. And this is really what we're focusing on in this chapter is how do we get people into those sales conversations? How do we get people talking to us into the buying mindset where they can be persuaded to make a purchase or at least trial our product and give it a shot to see if it solves their problem. Now, all too often what companies do is they only do this, but they kind of neglect the rest of the funnel because constantly pushing something like a demo, which is a free offer as a marketing tactic, is only going to be effective to an extent.

Now, at the very bottom of the funnel, we have paid off or unaware. So people that maybe aren't aware of your contract terms, they don't know about pricing negotiations. And really, this is the space of your account executives, the people that are going to put together the right proposal that will ultimately be agreed upon by the prospect. Now there is a small role that we can play in marketing here on the advertising side for things like retargeting and stuff. But it's primarily our sales that are going to have the most strength.

So this bottom of funnel, which is primarily where we're trying to promote or offer like or demo or trial or consultation, etcThe style and aesthetic of this type of marketing is not super artistic. It's not these off the wall advertisements that you see from creative agencies. It's less emotional. It can be somewhat emotional. It can be somewhat artistic. But first and foremost, it's rational.

The reason that it is rational is because what we're trying to do at the bottom of the funnel is drive short term decisions and responses. And the things that drive people to make short term decisions are really kind of rational choices. Now, in the long term, we're more focused on really embedding ourselves into the long term memory of people and associating our brand with some sort of category or buying situation. Give it some long term context. And in cases like this, at the top of the funnel marketing can be more creative, less rational, more emotional. But at the bottom, it's more, why should I act now? And what kind of benefit are you going to give me? In the next chapter, what we're going to do is we're going to get specifically into two very bottom of the funnel advertising types, which are going to be message and conversation ads.

Message Ads

Message and conversation ads are the ads that go directly to people's inboxes. Now, this is not to be confused with email within mail in LinkedIn Sales Navigator. What you're able to do is send a personalized, customized message that is kind of force fed to people's inboxes. This is different. This is more scalable. This is more automated. These are actual advertisements, not just messages that are coming from your sales team, and they're a little different from each other.

So conversation ads are basically a more advanced version of the message. And so what we're going to do is we're going to start with the message ad, because it's much more simple. Here is an example of a message chat. So you can see that I've just opened my LinkedIn and I'm in my inbox and I have some messages that are coming from connections in my network. And then occasionally what you'll see is you'll see something like an email, which is again just a message, but then you'll see something that says sponsor. This is the actual message and it says You've been chosen for free trial and it gets truncated and the rest of the information you can see on the right here. So there is a bold title, the subject line, if you will.

There's a Blue Call to action button, which I've customized. There's the sender, which is me, the body text. And then at the very bottom, the same call to action that was at the top also shows up in the bottom of the little arrow. And it's not really a button. It's just a sort of blue text that can be clicked. And when I click either at this button or this text at the bottom, a form opens up a lead capture form so that I don't have to send people to my website or my landing page. And the reason this is great is because it optimizes your conversions, because there's usually a drop off between when people click, when you're landing page loads and ultimately when they actually end up filling out the form.

So we want to reduce the friction as much as possible and this pop up form allows us to do that. So this is what a message ad looks like. Now. Why are message ads a good place to start? Now, a lot of people don't start here. This is actually considered a more advanced ad to some people. But if we really think about it, it's the simplest ad type. It may just be taxed. It's basically like writing an email. So you as the marketer, whatever your role is in the company, can put the entire ad together by yourself if you want it. You don't need a designer, you don't need a developer.

You don't need to change the website. You don't need to change the landing page. You can do it all within LinkedIn itself. And in that sense, it's just incredibly simple and quick to get launched. Now, the other key thing that I keep reminding you is you don't even need a website or a landing page. And because you don't you don't have to worry about conversion rate optimization. You don't have to worry about how well the website performs. Does it perform on mobile? It does. The form has too many fields. All of that just goes out the window. You don't need to worry about it.

Let's say you're a startup and you haven't built a website yet or you don't even have the money. You don't have $5,000 to build a WordPress website or whatever. You don't have the budget to have on bounce to create a landing page. Don't need to worry about it. This requires no fixed upfront cost. There's just the variable costs of sending the message. And LinkedIn takes care of all the recapture for you. Next, graphics aren't necessary. Now, ideally, you would have a banner ad that's next to the message ad, but you don't need it.

You can launch this campaign within a couple hours and not have to worry about working with any designer at all. One of the main reasons that I like to start with this is that it helps you focus on a compelling offer, which is the most important thing that you need to be doing at the bottom of the funnel. What is that offer that people are going to respond to, to take action that's going to entice them to have conversations with your sales team, consultants, whatever?

And in that sense, it's pretty much the most bottom of funnel advertisement type that we can have on LinkedIn. And with the philosophy of starting at the bottom of the funnel, it probably makes sense to at least think of this first. Now, it may not necessarily be the first ad that you launch. Like if you have a huge budget and you're planning out a macro campaign, it may not be the first that you go out of the gate with, but it's probably the first you need to think about because it's really what drives the sales pipeline.

Now, the previous message ad that I showed you got some results and I want to show you what those were. So we got 13 leads and the cost per lead was $22.12 Canadian. So I don't know what that is right now. Maybe $18 USD. We got over a thousand impressions, 665 clicks and an average click through rate of 56%. Now the click through rate of 56% sounds incredible. Well, it's actually too good to be true. This CTR metric is not reliable. Really, what it is, is it's more comparable to an open rate. So it means people actually open the message similar to opening an email.

You have to be a little careful sometimes with the variables and LinkedIn and deep dive to actually see what that means. Now the average CPM was $243 and the CPC was $0.43. Now let's get to the analysis of why this ad works. So what's at play here? What are the psychological principles or the direct response principles? Well, the first thing here is we have an offer or a special incentive visible before somebody even opens the message. So that's why perhaps we're able to get a 56% open rate. And we're going to talk about later some case studies about where having a special incentive is going to be one of the most important things.

So in this case, it's just a special invitation to a free trial. So we're not actually paying people for meetings or anything like that. We're not using Starbucks gift cards or any gimmicks. It's more an elite invitation. So you've been chosen for a free trial offer. Try talking to dictate. Now, the main point I want to take away from this message is that we are selling the offer, not the product. Now we can talk about the product, but it's of secondary importance.

We're leading with the offer itself, which is the special invitation to try talking to dictation. And that's one of the key principles and the bottom of funnel marketing. Sell the offer.

Now the other thing we're doing is personalization. Now the personalization is a bit superficial. Hi, your first name in this case should be the company name, which I've just set. That is my company name. So it sounds a bit silly.

Now that's personalization to one extent, but the personalization that's even more important is that it's relevant to them. So as a veterinarian, you've been invited to this. So that's what I'd be mindful of. Does your copy resonate with them specifically rather than just sort of broadcasting it to the world like spam? Next, I'm talking about some of the benefits of spending fewer hours on electronic health records. It is one of the main benefits of providing some proof. So the first type of proof from presenting here is actual research, a third party research from credible journals that they hopefully would trust to kind of prove that I can deliver on those benefits.

I'm also addressing objections, so you don't need a credit card. And one of the main objections is that it's going to work with every practice management software. Now, I did some research on core and read it and talked to veterinarians to figure out, well, why, why might people not try this offer? And those are some of the things that came up. Now I have more proof being presented here, but in this case, I'm not using broad based research. I'm using more anecdotal proof. It's social proof. It's a testimonial of somebody who successfully solved their problem using our product.

Now ideally what you do is you present the offer as the solution rather than the product, but, you know, work with what you got. And the other thing here is having a personal center. So at the bottom, it actually has my name. And you can see here it has my picture as well. Now, ideally, this would have come from another veterinarian, somebody that is trusted by the people that you're sending the message to. But sometimes if you need to move quickly, you just have to get it out the door.

Now, once you've started collecting the leads, how do you actually get access to them? Because the leads aren't going to go directly into your sales force, your Zoho or MailChimp, whatever you're using. So what you do is this is the new interface on LinkedIn, and you go down to the bottom here, which has assets, and one of the assets you can click is lead gen. Okay. This is going to give you access to legion forms, which you can see here. I have a whole bunch of lead gen forms and when I go in there I can click this button, which is download leads and that's going to give you an Excel file that you can then upload into your salesforce or wherever you're storing your prospects and your customers.

But eventually you're going to want to automate this. So in the beginning I would be agile. I would just manually download things. And then once you see that it's working and that this is advertising you want to keep doing. Then I would do an integration. Now there are some pre-existing integrations. So we got a converter here, we got HubSpot. Here's an example of when you go to the HubSpot page where you would download the LinkedIn integration, we got Marketo, which I've used before.

We got some Salesforce integrations. One thing that you may have to end up doing if your software doesn't exist on this list is set up a zipper integration. So that's one thing that I did. Well, I didn't actually set it up, but I used a zipper integration that my team set up so that the leads that are collected in LinkedIn are automatically fed into our CRM. Now, once you start launching your message ads, you're going to want to see how they perform. And this is what the campaign manager looks like. I want you to pay very close attention to this column chapter.

Now, this is one of the most important chapters to monitor that a lot of people miss. By default, it's going to say performance here. And that's going to give you some really useful information like the leads that are coming in, the clicks and stuff like that. But it's not going to give you the granular details. So in this case, the granular details we want are going to be when we select sponsored messaging. So then we're able to see very specific information like how many message clicks open, button clicks specifically. So not just all clicks, but button clicks, a click to open rate cost, percent cost per open average CPC.

And those details, that's going to be very important because I showed you earlier that things like seats are deceptive when we're thinking about message ads. So be very mindful of playing around with this column chapter. Now a few tips when it comes to messages at once. Again, S.T.A.R. is basically open range, so don't don't trust it. You have a number of variables you can use in the way that you use them if you put in the percentage sign like I've written here. Percentage time, percentage sign, first name, percentage sign. So the options you have are your first name, last name, job title, company name and industry. So all of those can be customized at scale.

In your message ads. One I'd be very mindful of is industry. Be very careful with using this because the industries that are available, LinkedIn are not necessarily the industries that your prospects will actually describe their industry. So for example, I work in the SaaS industry software as a service, but there is no SAS industry and LinkedIn. And this is similar to government classifications for industries that are kind of old fashioned, if you will, and not necessarily colloquial language that we use. So in my case, I have to go with either Internet or computer software.

Now, when I receive a message that says computer software or Internet, I don't think of it as spam because it just sounds fake to me. Nobody talks like that in my industry. Now the other thing you want to do is have a conversational tone, right? This message looks like it's coming from an individual, like it's a 1 to 1 conversation. Conversational writing tends to perform well when we're doing direct response, when we're doing salesy copy. So I would try to do that as much as possible. I would try to put a graphic to the side of your message ad because if you don't, your competitor might. And if they click it, they'll go to your landing page. But obviously it's not really going to be an option for you if you don't have the resources to put together a design or to put together a landing page.

The other thing to keep in mind is that it's not cost per click. You're paying a percent. So it's analogous to sending like a direct mail postcard. So let's say it costs you $3 to print and send a postcard. Well. In the case of LinkedIn, to send a message that might be $0.40. And it's much faster to get something like this out the door. But that changes the economics of how you think about message ads versus something like Google ads, which tend to be on a CPC basis. Now in the next chapter, what we're going to do is we're going to stay here in the message conversations, ads part, but we're going to deep dive into the conversation ads which are more advanced versions.

Message Ads Tutorial

This is a tutorial on how to create a message. First thing I'm going to do is go to Google and type in the LinkedIn campaign manager. I see the results, so I click it. I see this blue button click create. I'm going to create a campaign. I'm just going to go with the default campaign group. You could use a different campaign group or create a new group. One of the most important decisions is going to be what the objective will be.

And at the bottom of the funnel, in most cases, it is going to be lead generation. So I'm going to check that off in LinkedIn. You have to specify geographies, unlike Facebook, where you can type in worldwide here, you pretty much have to specify which regions or countries you're going to go after. Just for demonstration purposes, I'm going to say we're going to go after the United Kingdom in addition to the preset option here, which was the United States. You can also exclude biographies if you want it now. Who is your target audience?

In this case, it's already filled in with a specific job title. That's just because LinkedIn is guessing who I want to target based on previous campaigns. So what I'm going to do is just click the X here to exclude that. Now what you can do is simply search for whoever it is that you want to target. So in this case, maybe I want to go after product marketing managers. And it's going to give me some different options here. So member groups. Other member groups, company names. Okay, that's nothing that I want. So what I'm going to do is I'm going to get rid of the S and O. Here is what I'm looking for.

So a product marketing manager has a job title, so it'd be a very typical case of what you would do with the targeting. You would target a job title. The other thing that I would do is I would check to enable audience expansion and often I would use the exclude option to try to omit people that are either in human resources or in sales. So as an example, here, I would type in human resources. And Human Resources manager, you might put in other types of human resources job titles. But for demonstration, I would also want to exclude people in sales. So I would type in here something like account executive. So there's a bias in LinkedIn favoring people that are in H.R. in and sales because they tend to use LinkedIn much more frequently.

And unless your product or service caters to those people, you probably want to put them in the negative targeting. Now I'm going to go into more detail with the targeting options. But a couple of things I want to highlight here is what I showed was the most basic type of targeting you would do, which is you just do a search for something like a job title or a function such as marketing or human resources. But since we're at the bottom of the funnel, which you may want to do, is called a list upload. So there are two clusters of targeting here. There are audiences and audience attributes.

Audience attributes are actually the most basic and simple, even though it's the second option. And that's what we did here with the job title. But audiences, which are match audiences, this is a little more advanced. Now, at the bottom of the funnel, you may do a list upload. And what you would do is you would upload either a company list or a contact list. And at the bottom of the funnel, the ideal scenario is you're uploading a list. Has intent data backing it to show that there was buyer intent with specific companies and you would get that from a third party. So there is an advanced option that you would want to do here.

And the other advanced option that you might want to consider, since you're at the bottom of the funnel, is retargeting. So you would click retargeting. And what you may want to do is retarget people that watched a video. Or you may want to retarget people that visited your website, for example. So the idea is that people that watch the video or visit your website are more familiar with your product or familiar enough that they'd be ready to do something like get a demo, have a consultation, talk to your sales team, talk to a product specialist, something like that.

Now I'll go into more depth on the targeting options, but for simplicity, I'm just going to stick with product marketing managers and excluding these people in sales and H.R. So we would select here as the ad format message ad. And the other thing that you'll notice is I exclude enabling audience expansion because I want to have full control over who sees my ads. The other thing that I did was I'm including the audience network in most cases, but you can see here that for this particular use case with the message ads, I don't actually have that option. So because these are ads that go to people's inboxes, I can't take advantage of this where normally I would. So that we can set the daily budget.

I'm just going to say $50 per day. And you'll notice that we have very limited options in terms of optimization and bidding. And that's because when you send a message your charge percentage is similar to what you would have with direct mail. But what I do have control over is the amount that I'm willing to bid. So I'm going to put in a really low bid of $0.10. And you'll notice that LinkedIn will rebuttal with the minimum of $0.40. So I'm just going to say $0.41 just for fun to beat the competition. Okay. So we have our bid, we have our ad format, we have the targeting and we have the geographies for the targeting. So we'll click next.

So now the campaign's been created, but we haven't actually created the ad, sort of created the ad. You can click here or you can click here. And click the more image based one we might name that the ad message tasks the sender in this case is going to be me, which you might want to do is add a sender who is an influencer. So you could go to a tool like Spark Toro, form a little bit of a temporary partnership with an influencer who will send your ad, be the voice of your ad, the face of your ad. That could be very effective.

It's also effective just to get somebody in your company who maybe has more credibility with the target audience and the subject line. What you want to highlight usually is the special incentive or the invitation. So you might say invitation for top. CTOs or in this case, product managers. Or you would say $100 for leading. For top product managers. So basically the thing that's very enticing is what you want them to see. First off, when they see your message and you might say something like a high percentage sign, first name I'm inviting. Exceptional product. Marketing managers. To this. Demo to get $100 and give us honest feedback on our products. And then you might have like a full, a few bullet points like, um. Get x y. Something like sincerely.

Basically the message that is what is in it for me. Why should I respond to the special offer? And then you would select a call to action. So this might be like getting $100 and a demo to solve. Demo. You might want to tie it in to like the problem, like solve the problem. So you're your call to action instead. Could be something like. Solve a demo, something like that. Just a few different things to consider. The landing page. Now the call to action button is actually going to go to the LinkedIn lead capture form. It's not going to go to your landing page, but LinkedIn wants you to put in a landing page. It's going to be important if you choose to have an image next to the ad, next to the message tag. But that image is actually optional.

So in this case here, I'm just going to put in my LinkedIn page, you might want to put in your company page, you might want to put in a specific landing page on your website. Either of those is fine. Now, for the form that pops up here, you can either select a form that's already been generated like I did this. And all I have here is I collect the first name, which is a pre-populated last name populated email may or may not be populated with it. The other thing that you can do here is just create a new form, a new lead capture form, and you'll be able to put it in something like. Hundred dollar gift card for product.

Marketing managers offer details. Only 20 minutes of your time. Solve Problem a. These are just a few things to consider.

You have to put it in your privacy policy here and then you can put in different information you want to collect. So first name, last name, email address you can put in something like a company. I generally steer away from very lengthy lead capture forms, but, you know, that's my bias. You may have a place for collecting more information to hand off to the sales team. Usually I like to get as much information upfront when I'm targeting and building the list that I don't have to.

When I have the form where lengthy forms perhaps are more important is when you're focusing on inbound marketing through something like search engine optimization because you don't have full control over who's seeing your ads. With LinkedIn, you have very strong control over who sees your ads. You can also open ended customer questions here if you want to. This confirmation thing in the form is very important because it's a secondary call to action. So what you might have here is something like your common link. So that's basically once some people, once people submit the form, perhaps to do a consultation with me, they will automatically be directed to this thank you page, this thank you form where they can click the button to go to a page to actually schedule time on my calendar. So I might put something like schedule your free demo here.

And then you select what the button would be. So visiting the company website would make sense. Here to learn more. Another thing you might have is like watch a quick three minute demo video and then you would say view now and this could be a link to perhaps your YouTube. Or it could be linked to a video that's on a dedicated page on your website, perhaps even the homepage you could by default. You could even just send people to your homepage just so they're more familiar and nurtured along in terms of product education. So let's see here.

We got some sort of error, so we need to ask a question here. Tell me what you think. A B. It would hit create. So this is a short preview of what the ad looks like. What I'm going to do is click these three buttons and hit send a text message. Then I'm going to go to my LinkedIn to see what that message looks like. Oh, here it is in my inbox. Okay. So there you have it. There is the bold subject line at the top. It's truncated on the left. There's a button here and then there's a button down here. When I click it, it opens the form and then people are able to hit submit.

Conversation Ads

Conversation ads are very, very similar to me as jazz, but there are a couple of very important differences. The most important difference is that you can have multiple calls to action with conversation ads. In fact, you can have many different calls to actions that sort of create this tree of decisions similar to what you might see with a chat board, but not necessarily. You can set it up however you want.

The other key difference is that you can include an image in the ad itself, whereas with message ads, the image has to go to the side of the image in a conversation can be embedded right there below the text, for example. So here is an example of a conversation ad. This is an ad that I received from LinkedIn itself, from this individual from Grace, and it says, There's a bunch of text you can see the LinkedIn offer on the left here that shows up similar to how I received messages from people in my network.

And then the key thing that stands out here is there are three different calls to action. So I actually get to choose my own adventure here. Yes. Tell me more. Yes. Read the report or I'm unsure. All too often when I'm solicited by people, I'm given one option, which is, do you have time for a 15 minute call, a 30 minute call, a demo, whatever. Here, they're giving me some agency to make a decision, which is great. Now this hour is very exciting. And one reason is because of this case study. And the quotation here is how I generated five X returns from one leading conversation ads campaign. This comes from Jason of metadata.

Now, what does that actually mean? What were the results that Jason got from this? Well. First, What he did was he promoted a $100 DoorDash gift card for a demo. Now, this is very controversial. A lot of people disagree with this. A lot of big influencers in marketing hate the idea of paying people to get into a conversation with you. But the problem is, I've just seen so many case studies. I've done this myself where having some sort of offer, like giving people $100, $200 gift card, whatever, just gets results, it gets pipeline, it gets customers.

It doesn't just get people that are in the meetings just for the money for the most part, from my experience. I think one of the reasons it's very effective is not just that people value the money, they value the respect that you respect their time. Now, as someone who gets solicited all the time for people that want to be my partner, they want me to do a sales call like I have limited time. I'm a busy person, I'm an experienced person. So what I do is I listen to the people that respect my time and offer me money regardless of whether a hundred dollars makes a big difference to me or not.

And I think that's one of the psychological elements at play here. It's also just a way of standing out from the crowd. If you're being hit with three solicitations a day and one person offers you money, you're going to pay attention. So one of the most effective tools you can use at the bottom of the funnel is you have your main offer, which is like your demo or whatever. And then you couple it with a special incentive offer, which is like $100. Okay. So with Jason, he had an audience of 50,000, so that would be pretty typical for a link to a campaign, LinkedIn campaign, maybe you have 10,000, 100,000 people generally.

He spent about a quarter million dollars. The average cost percent was $0.30 to $0.70. That's pretty typical for a conversation ad or a message ad as well. 2000 demo requests. So MQ tells of 2000 pipelines over $5 million in pipeline, and then at the end of the day, $1.3 million in revenue. So that's pretty enticing, right? Just by using this one ad type, he spent a quarter million dollars and got over $1,000,000 in revenue. It's a pretty clear, strong return on investment, and that's perhaps rare in the marketing sphere where people are generating tons of Maxwell's tons of marketing captured leads, but they're not necessarily generating the real revenue.

And one way you do that is by promoting things like gift cards. So let's hear some advice from Jason and metadata. Okay. So pick the right sender. Now, I mentioned earlier how I sent an ad for my name. It would have been more effective if we had a celebrity that an influencer, perhaps, that the target audience respects. One way you can do that is by finding them on Spark Toro. I use that as a tool to find influencers, and maybe you can get some sort of partnership where they send the ad on your behalf and they get a percentage cut or they get some sort of fix on something like that.

Maybe your CEO has a lot of visibility, or maybe you just have someone in your company that has the same credentials as your target customer. So, for example, a chief marketing officer is probably better for them to send a message to marketers than the CEO. Or perhaps if you have a chief medical officer and you're trying to go after doctors and have the message come from that. The other thing is having the incentive in the pre header. So make it very obvious in the beginning on the left in the inbox that there's something in it for them. Social proof in the intro. So maybe there's a company that your target customers respect, that uses your product, will highlight, that shows how you understand the problem and have to solve it so clearly about the value proposition, the main benefit and playing for money grabbers using things like qualifying criteria.

Now I think this is good, but I wouldn't. I wouldn't overthink this. Often what I see in business to business is people try to fix things at the forum level. So there's a problem where they're getting a lot of bad leads and they think, okay, well, if we force people to put in a work email, for example, that we're going to get better leads. I prefer to fix things at the top of the funnel, at the targeting level, so that by the time they get to the form, there are they've already qualified. And I really, really think that when marketers try to fix things at the form level, that's really just a marketing strategy issue in terms of getting the targeting right. And that's particularly troublesome when you're doing this kind of inbound marketing where you're getting a lot of garbage leads from companies that are not big enough or are not a good fit.

But when you're doing outbound like this, less of an issue, however, you know, you can consider putting in qualifying criteria here if you are getting people that are just getting the meetings to get them cash and don't actually have any genuine interest in your product. Okay. So the main psychological reason that conversation ads work is because they give prospects agency, they give them choice. And we have a quotation here from Dr. Jonah Berger of the Wharton School, author of Contagious and Offer, author of The Catalyst, which is really what I'm highlighting here, is research and the catalyst.

So to avoid getting shot down, allow for agency, guide the path, but make sure people feel like they're still in control. So when you do a conversation and you're actually in control, you're deciding the menu of choices that are available, but it creates the illusion or a limited set of control to the prospect and people like that. Now, with conversation ads, you can add up to five calls to action. I would probably go with around three. You don't want to overload people with analysis paralysis. In the next chapter, what we're going to do is we're going to step away from the advertising world a bit and start focusing on our reach with LinkedIn Sales Navigator.

Conversation Ads Tutorial

Here's a tutorial on how to create a conversation ad. I'm the campaign manager. I'm going to see this blue button to create a new campaign. I'm going to leave it in the default campaign group hit next. The objective is going to be lead generation, which is usually what we're doing at the bottom of the funnel. I'm going to leave the geography as the United States.

I'm going to specify the targeting in this case. I'm going to ax this off and I'm going to go with something like the director of i.t. And we can see here that director of information technology is what LinkedIn calls this title. So I'm going to select that. I am not going to enable audience expansion. I'm going to select the conversation ad as the ad type. I would enable linking an audience network, but it is not an option for this on time. I'm going to lower the ad budget to $50 per day.

My bidding strategy is going to be based on the amount that I'm willing to pay to send my message to people's inboxes. You know, often with other ad types like images, LinkedIn will suggest a certain amount and it will also give a range that it recommends. But usually what you can do is put in a really low bid to find out what the actual minimum is that you can pay. Now, with LinkedIn message and conversation ads, what I find is that the default often is actually the lowest bid. So if I put in something like $0.10, you can see your bid must be at least $0.95.

And that's actually what LinkedIn is putting by default. But I like to just get in the habit of assuming that LinkedIn is wanting me to bid higher than I need to. So I would get in the habit of putting in a low bid, particularly when it comes to image and video ads. So we're going to leave it at the minimum here of $0.95. I'm going to hit next and save. I've created the campaign, but now there's the matter of actually creating the ads. So let's do that.

Choose the center test combo and leave the center for me. Select the lead gen form. So I'm just going to go with a pre-existing form that I created and you can create a new one if you want it to hit next. Now, the thing with conversation ads is not only are there multiple calls to action multiple buttons, but whenever you click one of these, you can then be triaged to another set of options. So if they answered yes to this, then you prompt them with another question so it can get pretty complicated. That's why generally I like to choose one of these pre-existing templates and go with, for example, drive trials and demos, which is something I would normally do in my situation, and then I would hit next after creating that template.

And you can see what the basic template looks like here. And then you can modify it. So hi there, first name and hi, my name is well maybe they don't care what my name is, so I might get straight to the point here. I'd like to delete all of this. I'd like to offer you $200 to get your input on our new A.I. product too. Solve your problem. And only one day. One day. And then I might have something like social proof testimonials. I might have something like research proof. I promise to deliver y results and x time, etc., etc. You can come up with whatever you want.

Now, the cool thing about conversation ads is you can add an image that will actually go into the ad itself and not just go next to the ad like commerce, say, or like message ads do. You can choose what your button text says. So it could be. Schedule your demo. And then it can open the Legion form. So this is showing the real power of conversation ads is the button. The call to action can go to the Legion form, which we saw with the message ads, but it can also show the next message. So they get prompted again with a message or can send people to the website.

Now for the main call to action, I wanted to open the login form. That's the main thing we want them to do, schedule the demo or the consultation. The second one might be something like Tell me more, or I like to do something like Connect, connect with me on LinkedIn. So this is a bit of a connection with me, LinkedIn. A little bit of a softer offer. And then I would just put in. My LinkedIn address here. Now you can add another button and I might say something like. Start a live chat.

And then what that would do is it would go to wherever on your website you might have a live chat, maybe you have a specific live chat that's dedicated to you or whoever is sending the message you could put in anything here, like learn more about this offer. And then what you could do is send them to a landing page that's devoted to this ad, catering to IT directors, and the special offer of $200 might have a picture of a visa gift card or something like that. Now, since I don't actually have a URL for this, I'm just going to delete it. But you can see on the preview on the right that it would show up here as a third option.

So what we're going to do is we're just going to go ahead with two calls to action and hit create. Okay. So we see we're getting an error here. Now, when you get errors with conversation ads, you would go to the view flowchart up at the top, right, to see where that error is. Now, the cool thing about the flowchart is it gives you this high level overview of the complexity and the triaging points that happen within the conversation ads. So we see here that this is where the error is: there's no URL. Okay.

So I would put something like this in here. There's no. You were all here either, so I might have put in. HGTV. Something like that. And hopefully we can see that it didn't solve all of our errors. And we have errors here too. So I fixed all of the errors just by putting in new URLs. You have the option of viewing the preview to see how all these triage points happen. What I'm going to do is I'm going to hit create. You see that it's automatically in draft, you can send a text message to myself. So we'll see what that test message looks like.

Go to my inbox. Well, here it is. Okay, so there are two calls to action buttons. I see some text here. I see that it shows up in my inbox as sponsored and I can click one of these to open the form or click this, which goes immediately to my LinkedIn page. Happens to be a broken URL, but you can put in your specific website, whatever. Now, after they click that, you see that I'm being prompted again with even more calls to action buttons based on the template that we chose.

LinkedIn Sales Navigator & Outreach

I highly recommend getting LinkedIn Sales Navigator. And this is true even if you're not a salesperson. If you were in marketing, I think it's incredible. I think LinkedIn Sales Navigator is one of the best, most reliable ways of getting up to date contact information, up to date lists, up to date leads that you can generate lists for.

Now, I've worked with list brokers, I purchased leads. I've done a lot of these different techniques, and sometimes they're hit or miss. But I would say that LinkedIn Sales Navigator is definitely kind of the default thing that should be in your roster. So what we're going to do is we're going to walk through Sales Navigator and how to use other software in conjunction with LinkedIn Sales Navigator to do a real outreach campaign, particularly based around account based marketing. So kind of the general approach that people often take with LinkedIn ads is they will create something like an e-book or a white paper and they'll put it behind some sort of capture form. So you have to put in your name and your email to get access to it.

The problem is that this is actually a very slow, incredibly inefficient way to collect leads. But really you're not collecting leads. What you're doing is collecting contact information, and it's much faster to get contact information by using LinkedIn sales navigator than running ads and creating ebooks and stuff. It's just very costly. It might cost you, I don't know, a typical ballpark might be $50 or something to generate leads that way.

Now, what I use is a three step outreach process. So the first is list building, second is automations, and the last here is personalized outreach. So list building really starts with creating the account list. And a lot of people know what they do and LinkedIn Sales Navigator is a go straight to creating a lead list. Don't do that. Start with the account list. It's more efficient that way. Then you can generate the lead list, then you can create an email list.

Now the cool thing about the email list is you can import it in the LinkedIn advertising and just target those individual emails or you don't even necessarily need an email list. You might just have a list of companies or a list of individuals and use that for targeting purposes. So when you're in LinkedIn ads, you can't actually target individuals. You can target based on variables like job title, seniority, etc. But if you use Sales Navigator in conjunction with LinkedIn Campaign Manager, then you can get down to the individual level, down to the individual company level. Okay, so once you've built the list, then we can think about automation. So we can automate things like LinkedIn visits.

So visits to people profiles, automate connection requests, automate messages, and we can automate emails as well. What I'd be very cautious about is automating messages on LinkedIn. I think it can seem very spammy and I'd be very worried about it, particularly if you're going after enterprise accounts or really high value accounts where they're bombarded with spam anyways and it's just not going to be super effective. The last step here is to personalize outreach. So this is less automated, less scalable where you're going to need to collaborate with the sales teams more. And that's going to be doing things like email.

So using the credits that you get through LinkedIn Sales Navigator to send individualized messages, we're going to do individual personalized emails, particularly to high value partners like influencers or to high value accounts. We're going to do things like direct mail and other sort of outreach techniques that are more custom. So to start, what we do is we go to the sales navigator, which looks like this, and we start creating a countless. So I would click this account countless times.

You can see I have a bunch of a countless here and I've named them based on keywords and size of company, etc. and there's a limit to a thousand and in for each list, but you can see some of them. I only have maybe around 501 of these, I only have 99. So that's fine. You can build a whole bunch of a countless if you need more than a thousand. So what we would do is we do a search, so an advanced search that shows these different filters. And it's cool now that we have a new interface for the searches and we can actually specify annual revenue, which is great.

Now, I don't know where LinkedIn gets that information, how reliable it is, but generally I start with something like headcount and I say, okay, we're going to target companies that have maybe 50 to 200 employees. We're going to add in may be small companies, maybe bigger companies than that. We can put in other information here or like department headcount, if that's more relevant as headquarters location. A lot of these I don't usually use, but I'm highlighting with these arrows here the ones that I find the most important industry incredibly important and technology is also a very useful thing.

So for example, if your product is only compatible with certain CRM, SMS or certain ERP, you want to specify that if you can add it, it's very difficult to get this through other targeting sources or other list brokers. So take advantage of it while you can. Now once you've compiled your lists using these search filters. So I had a revenue 2.5 below 100 million. You're going to get a list of companies here. You're going to check them off. You can check off all the people visible on the screen. Then you're going to save the list and name it. So you don't want to do all that effort and have it get lost. So the next stage, once you have the account list is, then you do the lead list.

Now the problem with LinkedIn Sales Navigator is it's going to try to force you to generate lead lists by default. You want to keep negating that and clicking the account. But once you've completed the account list creation, then you can go to sort of this default option, which is the lead, the lead list and the lead search. So in the lead search, you can see we have various options here. So functions like marketing or sales, job title, very important seniority, very important years in company, maybe in born years and current position maybe important.

We got school years of experience. Industry could be quite important, but the most important factor here is down here, hidden on the bottom right here is the countless is are they in the account list that you're targeting? So if you're doing account based marketing, you want to target leads, individuals, personas that are within that account. And that's why you need to create the countless first. So once you have your lead, less. Based on those accounts or not?

I mean, you could go after just individuals if you want and skip the account stage, but it's more scalable if you start with accounts. What you can do is you can extract the email. So I use this tool called Scrap Dinero, which is basically a chrome extension. I go into the extensions and I click scrap dot IO email finder, and then it's going to pop up a thing like this. So what I can do is I extract the lead list and then export it to scrap that IO. And what it's going to do is it's going to pull all the emails from those people.

Now it's not going to get all of them, but it's going to get a good chunk enough that you can then go into scrap that I go and download an Excel file which you can see here. So what you would do is you'll have your email list on the left and you can name it whatever you want, directors of it, for example. And above that I have here you're going to get the listed individuals. I've censored them here with their titles. So KTO, director of technology, vice president of information technology. It's going to show me if the emails have been verified or not. It's going to give me their emails and then I can go here to download and download as a CSP. And the other thing that I can do here is I can choose whether or not I want leads that don't have emails that were not found or not.

And I can also do that at the export level when it is exported from sales navigator into scrapped audio. So that's going to give me an email list. Now the question is, what do you do with that email list? Well, you can import it into your called email tool.

So the example I'm using here is lamb list. You might use mail shake. If you're a larger company, you're going to use something like a sales loft or outreach, which is what I was using in San Francisco. And what you would do is you would go to this upload CC option so that the CSV file that you download it from scrap that I oh you upload in your cold email tool, you can build a series of campaigns around those lead lists that you compile.

The other thing you want to do is you want to validate emails so that the bounce rate, the rejection rate is not very high and your deliverability is going to improve. So I use this tool called bouncer to verify the emails. Now bouncer integrates with LEM lists so you can see the limbless integration. That's the reason that I'm demonstrating that here. And again, you can either upload the file or what I do is I just pull the list that's already been imported in the lemme. So the next thing that you do is you want to set up your automations. So there are different things that you can automate.

You can automate links in visits, invitations in messages. I will be very careful with the messages part, but I think automating a linked-in visit is a very kind of harmless thing to do and invitations would probably be pretty similar. The other cool thing is that when you use a tool like lemons, you can test entire sequences. So the sequence might be like a cold email linked to a LinkedIn message or multiple emails and follow ups, and you can test the entire sequence against another. So here I have a sequence only. Sequence B when you use something like ActiveCampaign or a lot of these tools that have a B testing capabilities, they won't let you test the entire sequence. They only let you test individual emails or messages. So that's one cool feature that we have here at last.

Now you can also test the individual messages as well. So here I have a macro test of A and B, but then I have a micro test that's just step three testing. Email A versus email B. So, for example, sequence A, you might talk about one benefit in sequence B, you talk about a different benefit and see which one performs better. And then here you're testing individual body copy or individual offer, something like that. Now what I have here is step one is visit the LinkedIn profile. I have a delay of a day and then I will link you to an invitation. Then I wait three days and I send a cold email, which ideally is a little bit warmed up because of the LinkedIn interactions. Okay.

Key things to consider. You want to limit the number of LinkedIn automations in email so you don't. You don't want to come out of the gate sending 500 emails a day and LinkedIn automations. It's not going to bode well, not going to be sustainable. So you kind of want to ramp your volume up. So you might start with 30 emails a day, go up to 70, and maybe you get around 100, $200 or 200 emails a day. And if you need more, well, you can set up multiple emails. You can work with SendGrid or whatever, work with your team to have unique IPS and stuff some, some ways around the limitations there. When you're first starting to call email, use a different domain.

So if it's company dot com, you want to go with a company dot org and you know John or company dot org don't don't put your main domain at risk and you want to warm up your new email address. So if it's a fresh email, don't use the built in warm up process. So companies like Ally must have this thing called lean warm, which will sort of send and receive emails to make you look credible. Okay. So I'm going to talk about some cool email tips now. This is very important because. With LinkedIn. We're not just thinking about LinkedIn ads. We're thinking about outreach. We're thinking about campus marketing. We need to understand that when we're at the bottom of a funnel, we need to be seamlessly integrated with the sales team.

And this is something that a lot of business to business marketers are realizing now is they need to align with the sales team. So understanding things like cool email is very important, even if you're just focused on LinkedIn marketing. So to understand one of the main mistakes that people make, we need to think about what they do. Usually what they're doing is they're aggressively pushing to get meetings. So, hey, this is Billy. Here's my product. Do you have 50 minutes per call? You have 30 minutes to call. Would you like to do a demo?

Way too aggressive. Don't ask for a meeting and you're cold emailing. It's a huge turnoff. I get a whole bunch of these per day. Don't do it. And it's also validated by research. So we have ongoing research based on 300,000 emails. You are two times more likely to book a meeting during a cold email when asking your prospect for their interest versus asking for time. So essentially what they're saying is you're more likely to get a meeting if you don't ask for a meeting, because the problem when you ask for a meeting is you're kind of being selfish. You're kind of saying, Well, this is what I want, rather than trying to give them something.

Our bonus tip here based on Gong Research, don't talk about return on investment ROI in your initial email. It's too high level. It's too far removed. I think a huge mistake that people make in business to business marketing is they think that talking about high level benefits like saving time, making more money, getting more return on investment is what prospects wanna hear. They don't really want to hear that. In most cases. They want to hear more about the functional details of how you're able to accomplish the outcome that I want to. And that means moving from kind of high level benefits to lower level functional details about what your product actually does or what your service actually does.

Do not ask for a meeting right away. Do not talk about Roy right away. All right. Next, we have some cold email tips from Harvard Business Review. This comes from Tucker Max. So, number one, tailor the message to the recipient. So it may not necessarily be the individual. That's great if you're targeting high value accounts or influencers, but if you're trying to do it at scale, it may mean tailoring the message to a group of people that have a certain designation or that meet certain criteria. You also want to validate yourself. So maybe you were featured on Fox News. Maybe you have a Harvard degree. Maybe people know who your partner is in the business.

Do some sort of validation, alleviate your audience's pain, or give them something they want. So that could be an incentive. That could be. That's my recommendation. Not it's about having the incentive, but it could just be the benefit of your offer, for example. Keep it short, easy, and actionable. Now, be cautious about this because the word short is subjective, right?

So based on long research, what we're talking about here is 30 to 150 words. Now, if it's too long, it's kind of spammy. But if it's too short, you're not giving enough context.

You're not giving me enough information to validate why I should respond to you. But if you give a little bit of details about what you do, then that's good. And that can be done in 30 to 150 words and be appreciative and a little vulnerable. So you need to take a little bit of a submissive role and a less dominant role and put them in the action seat, make it seem like they're in control, which again aligns with our concept of agency that we talked about earlier. Okay. So the third step now, I talked about the three step process for outreach.

The last one here is the personalized outreach. So stuff that's less scalable, less automated. And within LinkedIn Sales Navigator, we have some cool features. So one is we can see which of our leads in our lists are posted on LinkedIn in the past 30 days and we can have our sales team or our SDR, BTR team comment on those posts and interact, build rapport with them. We can also send these in mail so we can send a message here, put in a subject line, put in a message that's more tailored than we would be able to do with the automations that we talked about earlier.

In the next chapter, we're going to talk about the most common types of ads. They're very similar to what you see on Facebook feeds. And these are the image and video ads.

Image Ads 1

Image and video ads are typically where people start when they get into LinkedIn advertising. I didn't start with them in this Book because what we're trying to do is build a full funnel campaign. And I wanted to start with the most bottom of funnel ad types that I could think of, which are the messaging conversation ads and ones that didn't require a lot of resources. But when you start producing images and videos, you need to involve designers. You need to get more sign offs.

You can't just sort of jump into it. So here is an example of what an image ad looks like. This is one that I developed. You can see that there is the company logo and the company LinkedIn page shows up at the top. This is something you want to be mindful of if you're not very active on your LinkedIn company page, I think that's fine. But you want to at least make sure that your brand design, your banner image, reflects the positioning of your product and you want to make sure that you're using the appropriate company page to advertise from.

The other thing I want to point out here is LinkedIn gives you a lot of space to write text here. All too often what companies do is they just put in one sentence or two sentences, which does not really make sense to me, because if you were paying for that ad space, you want to fill it as much as possible so that those that are interested in consuming more information can do so within the ad itself. All too often what marketers are trying to do is sort of artificially inflate the click through numbers by.

Saving the extra information or the juicy information for when you get to the Web page. The problem is fewer people are going to click. Fewer people are going to consume the content. So I'd put as much as possible into the text above the image. The other thing I want to point out here is I put a lot of text into the image itself here, and that's a decision that's up to you. From a creative and communications perspective. However, LinkedIn is much more flexible now.

I believe Facebook is starting to get more flexible in this regard, but I'm far more likely to get my images ads accepted by LinkedIn rather than going through the bureaucratic hassle of running these types of ads on Facebook. So even though they do look very similar to Facebook, you can probably get away with more on LinkedIn. So what I'm doing here is I'm just asking the question to them, to the audience, and I'm calling out to the audience of that. A veterinarian in this case, not a veteran. I have a sign up form at the bottom to go to the pop up for Legion.

I'm calling out what the offer is in this title. So I'm putting it in square brackets and there's a lot of creative choices you can make. But basically this is what it looks like. You have the title at the bottom, you have the image, and then you have a bunch of text. Now. The approach that a lot of people take with LinkedIn ads when they first get started is they'll create image ads, and the image ads are promoting an e-book or a white paper, and they have the image of the ebook or the white paper. But this is just generally a bad approach. Now, there are exceptions. There are cases where this might make sense.

You know, maybe if you only have five potential customers and they're, you know, super high value accounts and you want to see if they're engaged, then, okay, I could see you doing this. Or if your e-book is more focused around being a buyer's guide rather than just knowledge, then okay, that's something where you might want to have some sort of sign up form or gating process so that you can hang off those leads to an SDR. But in general, don't do it. There are far better ways to generate lists. I will walk you through how to do that with LinkedIn Sales Navigator, and here's one of the reasons that you don't want to do this.

And this is a quotation from James Anderson of the Kellogg School of Management. 70% of the leads generated by marketing tend to be ignored by Salesforce, and the average yield from leads are hovering around one and 2%. So basically what this is telling us is that whatever marketing is doing to generate leads, which is often promoting things like white papers and ebooks, it's not working. Sales doesn't want those leads. They don't want to talk to those leads. So let's stop calling those leads and instead let's call it what it is, capturing contact information which can be done through a list, broker or through compile. Compiling your own list. Okay. So here are some examples of how to do bottom of funnel image ads.

Now, these are not necessarily the approach that you're going to want to take later in the mid and upper funnel when you're talking about product education, problem education. But at the bottom, when you're really trying to get people into sales conversations or signing up for things like free trials, this is what you want to do. What you want to do is emphasize the offer. The incentive and or the outcome that you're promising, ideally that centered around the offer itself. What is the outcome of using the offer of signing up for the free trial, for example?

And often what people do instead is they create an entire ad that is talking about the product. But then the call to action is the offer, like the free consultation, the demo, while the ad itself ideally talks about the offer so that the call to action is aligned with what the rest of the message is in the air. Now, the best example that I could find lately on my LinkedIn feed was this one from Quartz Network. Now, I don't know what they do, but I find their offer very compelling. Get six free meetings with qualified executive buyers. You can see how this isn't talking about the company. It's not talking about the product.

It's just saying here is an outcome that we're promising and we're offering it for free as part of our offer. It's very empathetic. It's talking to the needs of the prospect rather than just being kind of internally focused on our company and our product. The other thing I want to call out here is this is one of the few examples where they're using what's called a carousel ad, where you have multiple images that you can scroll through. Personally, I haven't had a lot of success with these.

I think they generally have a good place probably in the mid and upper funnels when you're focused on education. But I thought this was just such a good example of copywriting and positioning the offer that I couldn't help but leave it in. Now, in most cases, at the bottom of the funnel, you can probably get away with what's called just a single image ad. But if you want to experiment with carousel ads, that's fine. Obviously, it seems to be working for them now.

Another compelling thing to do with your images that a lot of people don't use has an image of the incentive. So the incentive here is getting an iWatch. So let's put that image in there. And a lot of people say, oh, why are we focusing on the incentive? You know, we're just going to get people that just want the iWatch. They don't care about the product. Well, maybe some of them will be in that situation. But for the most part, if you're targeting it, right, if you're hurting the right people and you put in some qualifying criteria if you want, like they have to belong to certain types of companies or certain seniority, then it's a win win for everyone.

They get the iWatch and you get the meeting that one way or another, you're paying for the meeting whether you're giving the money to the prospect or you're giving it to LinkedIn for advertising. And you're probably going to get a much higher response rate by doing that so you can spend less on the advertising. Now, in this case, there's not actually an ad. This is just an image that they posted, but it could easily be run as an ad. And I think it would be very compelling and this type of thing is very successful with enterprise marketing, mid-market marketing, etc.

Now the other example we have here is Hootsuite. So what are they talking about in the ad? It's not Hootsuite. It's all about Hootsuite. 30 day trial. Now, an ad like this is going to work if you know what Hootsuite is. And they have a very strong brand. People are also familiar with what the product does, right? It does social media, management, etc. So an ad like this works in the context of other people being familiar with what you do, but they're just not necessarily educated on the fact that you have a 30 day trial.

Now, this is compelling because a lot of trials these days are only seven days, 14 days, and it's like, Oh, I can try Hootsuite stress free for 30 days. Okay, I'll sign up for it. Credit card companies are very good at this. Banks are very good at this. So earn up to $3,000 cash bonus. Again, very focused on the incentive on the offer. When I was in Canada, I was bribed to switch banks or to set up a bank account, not necessarily to switch by being offered a free iPod. So I did it.

I took the iPod sign up for the account, and I've been a customer ever since. On the Canadian banking side, another example here is an ad where we focus a copy basically on what the outcomes are from the offer, from the demo. So you're going to learn how to achieve 0% commission to extra revenue to your customer base, etc., etc. Again, the benefits, the walk away ways of doing the demo or the offer itself. Here's another example. Receive $100 welcome credit on government unlimited plan. So U.S. sellers are not coming out of the gate talking about who they are and what they do. They're coming out of the gate talking about a $100 welcome credit, which is the kind of focus you want to have at the bottom of the funnel incentive center focused.

Offer focused. Another thing to consider is having specific or unique offers instead of just doing the generic demos or talking to sales. Some examples of this is when you're targeting the Amazon audience. For example, you can say our free Amazon brand analysis. So that's very compelling, right? Because it's not just spam, it's something that's been tailored to the audience. So similar to what we're talking about with cold emails where you don't want it to come across as spam. You want to feel at least some degree of personalization, whether it's at the individual level or just at the group level.

Hey, this is saying this is for me and it's not just for anybody. Another example here is Rackspace request, your Microsoft cybersecurity assessment. Now, it's not just any old generic demo. And the last example we have here, innovative solutions request a no cost well architected review. Now, in cases like these, competitors are probably doing the same thing. At least some of them are probably offering a well architected review. They also might offer something like a microsoft cybersecurity assessment, but at least something like this is more tailored and feels more special than just sort of some generic run of the mill offer. Now, a couple of things I want you to note here.

One is you do want to give people the option to contact you. So generally, even when you're promoting something like a demo or you're focusing on a trial, a lot of the people that are going to become high value accounts will want to go straight to contact us. So you want to make sure your contact information is readily available wherever you can put it. The other thing I want to call out, which I've done personally, but I've also seen very successful empirically looking at the data of studies, or at least one study that I looked at is having logos of credible companies included in your imagery. So here we have a well.

So a lot of credibility here is achieved by picking off existing brands. And you see that with Rackspace here.

Not only is Rackspace a good brand, but they're also leveraging the Microsoft brand just as innovate is leveraging the Amazon brand. Another thing to consider is having a low commitment offer. So asking somebody to get on the phone for 30 minutes or even 15 minutes, which is better, but still perhaps a bit of a commitment. What you might want to do is offer something that is a low bar entry point. So, for example, the Dobie here has taken a three minute interactive tour. You watch the interactive tour, there may be some sort of gating to get access to it. And then what Adobe probably does is hands those leads off to an SDR who then tries to set people up

with a one on one meeting.

I had a colleague of mine who's very successful using a method like this, so a demo overview video that segued it into a one on one meeting and that's how they generated the pipeline. Another example that I have here is just signing up for a free trial. A free trial is generally a pretty low commitment offer, especially if it's just sort of a self-guided experience or a product led growth experience. And then it just leads to a low friction sign up form within LinkedIn itself. There's no need to go to a landing page. There's very little commitment here.

Now, a lot of people are going to say, well, they're so low on commitment. No, those people aren't going to be qualified. So what you're better off doing, they'll say, is sending people to your home, your website, so that they sign up for the demo to trial, whatever their. The problem is that you get, based on LinkedIn's own data, three times as many conversions. By having the native form within LinkedIn now, will a handful of those people be less qualified? Sure. But the absolute number of qualified leads you're going to get by using the native form is going to be higher, even though the percentage is going to be lower.

And this is one of the critical mistakes that I often see in marketing is there's too much obsession with the percentages. You need to be more interested in the absolute. Is the absolute market size big enough is the absolute number of qualified leads. Even though you're getting more garbage leads. And the other problem I see, and I repeat this point over and over is that don't you don't need to fix everything at the form level, fix things at the upper end of the funnel when you're doing your targeting so that you don't have to go in here and make sure that people have to are forced to put in their work, emails are forced to provide the phone number and all this qualifying information. Okay. So if we look at the ad that I ran earlier for that free trial, we got six leads at a cost of $28 Canadian per lead. So that's even less when we're looking at that.

In terms of U.S. dollars, 1700 impressions, 31 clicks at an average click through rate of 1.77%. So a click through rate of 1.77% is very high. For LinkedIn, we would expect something like 0.4%, maybe 0.5%. So given how exceptionally high that is, our cost per lead would probably go down if we switched from CPC to CPM because when we're getting clicks very effectively, we're getting a high percentage of clicks from our impressions. We don't want to be charged for the clicks. We want to be charged for the impression. So even though I recommend starting with cost per click because it's more conservative, safer to control if you're seeing good results in terms of engagement, then you want to switch to CPM.

Now the best way to assess engagement is to look at click through rate. That's the most obvious way to do it. It's not the only way to do it. LinkedIn is not going to give you your ad relevance score. It's something that is behind the scenes, but you can estimate or have some gauge of how good it is by looking at something like CPR. In a case like this. I have a very high relevance score. I can imply that. So I want to switch to a CPM bidding structure.

Now, the other key thing I want to point out here is you can spend all day trying to get your copywriting perfect, trying to get your images perfect. But ultimately, success is going to be dictated probably by more strategic considerations, which is going to be the target. And if we look at these two ads that I ran, I was getting leads four, it looks like around $14 for this one and around $10 for this ad here. So pretty good from a CPA perspective. Now that that's kind of a superficial leading indicator, not necessarily a hard metric like revenue, but it's a good starting point.

And one of the keys to success here was that the targeting was based on a list that I purchased. So I paid around $300 for a list, maybe $250 from doing a Google search. I imported it into LinkedIn, and had a very high match rate. I think it was over 90%, which is much higher than you would normally expect. And that's because the targeting was so good, the relevancy score was good, the cost per lead was low and the click through rate was quite good as well. So again, a case where you might want to switch to CPM bidding.

The other key thing here is that I'm testing the offer and this is something that a lot of business to business marketers don't spend enough time doing. It's very easy on LinkedIn to test your imagery and your ad itself. But one of the things that's really going to up your performance is changing what the offer is. So, for example, I tested here a free quote, price quote versus a get your question answer. So a free answer to the question. And surprisingly, the free price quote one actually outperformed, even though I expected it to be a more bottom of funnel thing that would appeal to fewer people. So we're going to take a look at this ad.

It comes from being smart. She is now smart. She's a good brand. I'm sure it's probably a good product. I haven't used it myself, but I just want to critique this ad and I want you to think about what may be a potential issue with this ad.

Conclusion

And as you scale up your marketing, a big question you should be asking yourself is should I be focusing on retargeting or lead generation? Now what most businesses do is they default to lead generation. There's been a colossal problem in the marketing world where marketing is generating all these leads and very, very few of them are translating to sales.

Very few are translating to actual sales conversations. So most of those leads are basically garbage. So to answer this question, let's go to the original purpose of lead magnets. Why do we generate lead magnets in the first place? These things like ebooks, reports, booklets. ET cetera. Well, the purpose of these lead magnets was to identify the subset of people who have the problem you solve so that you can nurture them. So basically, we're able to isolate a smaller group out of the larger audience that is worthy of our attention, worthy of putting energy into.

But one of the problems we've run into is that lead magnets are not actually doing a very good job of doing that. Now, basically what's happened is marketing departments are generating leads for the sake of generating leads. How do we maximize the number of leads? So what they're doing is they're changing the nature of the lead magnet. It's not what's going to be best to select the people that have the highest probability of buying from us. It's more what's going to have mass appeal in the market. So the whole function of a lead magnet has completely changed.

The other key thing that has happened is technology has changed. We no longer need to generate leads to identify people that have an interest in what we're selling. And one of the reasons is because what we can do is run video ads and we can say, okay, let's retarget the people that watch 50% of the video, three minutes of the video, 75% of the video, whatever. And then we don't need to gate the video. We don't need people to actually become a lead to watch the video. We can advertise the video itself. So with all these problems and all these changes that are happening, this raises the question should we do retargeting or should we do lead generation? So what's the argument for retargeting?

Well, the big argument is that it creates less friction. People don't need to submit a form, they don't need to put in their email, they don't have to put in their phone number, etcetera. And basically the idea is that's going to generate more customers. In the end, we're able to hit and influence more people. More people are going to watch our webinar, more people are going to watch your video, more people are going to watch our ad, But what's the argument for lead generation? Well, one of the strongest arguments is that the cost per impression, the CPMs are cheaper with email. So if we're able to capture people's email and nurture them over time, we're going to be able to hit them at a higher frequency, at a lower cost than we would with retargeting, because retargeting CPMs are higher than regular CPMs.

So we're paying a premium to amp up the frequency. So I just did some quick math here. As an example of a campaign. Let's say we're trying to influence one person with 20 touches. So basically a frequency of 20. We want them to see our ad or email, whatever, 20 times. How much is that going to cost with retargeting? Well, with just retargeting, you're looking at $0.33 to influence one person with lead generation, that's over $10. So this is a huge difference. So what are the assumptions I'm making here?

Well, the assumption here is that the email CPM is 133 $1.33. The CPM with niche retargeting is $35, which is typically what we would find on something like Facebook. And I'm saying that a normal non retargeting CPM is $15 because that's how we start the campaigns. We don't start with retargeting, we start with just influencing the large audience group. And then I'm assuming that it costs about $10 to generate a lead. Now if your lead price is even higher than that, it's typical in business to have around $50. Then you can see that the argument for retargeting gets even stronger. But if your lead is able to get lower, let's say below $2, then the argument gets a little bit stronger in favor of lead generation.

Here you can see how some of the math did, but there are some other considerations that you need to factor in. One is retargeting gets cheaper over time because the larger your retargeting group is, generally speaking, the cheaper it's going to be to influence that group with your ads. But you could also make the argument that as your email plan gets bigger, the cost per email address in your count is also going to be cheaper. Other things to consider is the price of cold email. So you may not necessarily need to do lead generation to nurture people through email. You could just go directly to them.

If you purchase a list or compile the list exported a list from LinkedIn Sales Navigator, for example. Uh, then you're able to take advantage of the cheap CPMs with email without necessarily generating the lead. But Of course that's not going to be possible in certain situations such as business to consumer, depending on the legalities of your region. Now another thing is if you have SDRs or account executives involved, their time is going to be very expensive. So that's going to really increase the price to acquire a customer.

And the other thing you need to consider is are you going to go with a higher frequency? Because 20 touches may not be enough to acquire customers. And if you're going to double that, then you can see that the fixed cost of lead generation becomes less important because we're dealing more with the variable expense of frequency and CPMs.

www.ingramcontent.com/pod-product-compliance
Lightning Source LLC
Chambersburg PA
CBHW071600150726
48000CB00004B/1541